Understanding the structure of English

Understanding the structure of English

Joseph E. Littlejohn
Southeastern Oklahoma State University

Winthrop Publishers, Inc.

Cambridge, Massachusetts

Library of Congress Cataloging in Publication Data

Littlejohn, Joseph E
    Understanding the structure of English.

    Includes bibliographical references.
    1.   English language—Grammar—1950–   I. Title.
PE1112.L54   428'.2   77-1910
ISBN 0-87626-891-2
ISBN 0-87626-890-4 pbk.

© *1977 by Winthrop Publishers, Inc.*
   17 Dunster Street, Cambridge, Massachusetts 02138

10 9 8 7 6 5 4 3 2 1

To Margaret, Karen, and Amy

contents

To the teacher   xi

**Introduction: Understanding the structure
   of the English language**   1

Making Grammar, 1   Some Things to Think
About, 2   Language and People, 4   How to
Make Grammar, 5   Getting Started, 6   The
Plan of This Book, 8

1 An introduction to the sounds of English   10

A. Background Data, 10   B. Making Grammar, 15
C. Grammar and People, 15   D. Evaluating
Grammar, 17

2 An introduction to units of meaning in English   19

A. Background Data, 19   B. Making Grammar, 23
C. Grammar and People, 23

**3 An introduction to characteristics
   of parts of speech**   26

A. Background Data, 26   B. Making Grammar, 30
C. Grammar and People, 33   D. Evaluating
Grammar, 33
       Parts of Speech in English by Waldo E. Sweet

4   **An introduction to basic sentence patterns**   **37**
A. Background Data, 37   B. Making Grammar, 40
C. Grammar and People, 40   D. Evaluating
Grammar, 42
Constituent Structure *by Philip S. Dale*

5   **An introduction to the basic function of
pitch in speech**   **49**
A. Background Data, 49   B. Making Grammar, 51
C. Grammar and People, 51

6   **An introduction to the basic function of
stress in speech**   **53**
A. Background Data, 53   B. Making Grammar, 55
C. Grammar and People, 55

7   **Expansion of basic sentences**   **57**
A. Background Data, 57   B. Making Grammar, 60
C. Grammar and People, 61

8   **Combining basic sentences**   **63**
A. Background Data, 63   B. Making Grammar, 66
C. Grammar and People, 66

9   **Summary of problems 1 to 8**   **68**
A. Background Data, 68   B. Making Grammar, 68
C. Grammar and People, 69

**Getting technical: terminology relevant to
problems 1 to 9**   **70**

10   **An introduction to the nature of the English
writing system**   **75**
A. Background Data, 75   B. Making Grammar, 78
C. Grammar and People, 79

Within the framework   **80**

11 **An introduction to sound-change in English**   **82**
        A. Background Data, 82   B. Making Grammar, 89
        C. Grammar and People, 89

12 **Some details of nouns, verbs, adjectives,
        and adverbs**   **91**
        A. Background Data, 91   B. Making Grammar, 93
        C. Grammar and People, 94

13 **Other parts of speech**   **96**
        A. Background Data, 96   B. Making Grammar, 99
        C. Grammar and People, 99

14 **Noun phrases**   **101**
        A. Background Data, 101   B. Making
        Grammar, 102   C. Grammar and People, 102

15 **Verb phrases**   **104**
        A. Background Data, 104   B. Making
        Grammar, 107   C. Grammar and People, 107

16 **Noun functions**   **109**
        A. Background Data, 109   B. Making
        Grammar, 111   C. Grammar and People, 111

17 **Complexity in sentence structure**   **113**
        A. Background Data, 113   B. Making
        Grammar, 115   C. Grammar and People, 115

18 **Deletions**   **117**
        A. Background Data, 117   B. Making
        Grammar, 120   C. Grammar and People, 120

19   **Underlying meaning in sentences**   **122**
A. Background Data, 122   B. Making
Grammar, 124   C. Grammar and People, 124

20   **Analysis of literal word-meaning**   **126**
A. Background Data, 126   B. Making
Grammar, 129   C. Grammar and People, 130

21   **The problem of nonliteral statements**   **131**
A. Background Data, 131   B. Making
Grammar, 133   C. Grammar and People, 133

22   **An introduction to speech contexts**   **135**
A. Background Data, 135   B. Making
Grammar, 136   C. Grammar and People, 137

23   **The basis of traditional grammar**   **138**
A. Background Data, 138   B. Making
Grammar, 142   C. Grammar and People, 143

24   **Revising traditional grammar**   **144**
A. Background Data, 144   B. Making
Grammar, 146   C. Grammar and People, 147

25   **The premises of two modern grammars**   **148**
A. Background Data, 148
The Structural Revolution *by Miriam Goldstein
Sargon*
**A Transformational Approach to Sentence
Structure** *by Ronald W. Langacker*
B. Evaluating Grammar, 173   C. Grammar and
People, 173

26   **The value of grammatical study**   **174**

Some more technicalities   **175**

to the teacher

There are today many different ways of analyzing the structure of the English language, such as traditional grammars, structural grammars, transformational grammars, to name only the most widely mentioned kinds.

And most books about the structure of English are explanations of one or more of these grammars. These books are deliberately designed to help students learn how a specific grammar works.

Understanding the Structure of English is deliberately designed to help students learn to think about how the structure of the English language works. It is not a presentation of a specific grammar of English.

It is a series of twenty-six "problems," each of which asks students to consider certain questions about an aspect of language and to gather data, to analyze, to explain, and to write about language. Many of the questions have no right answers, but I believe they are all worth thinking about.

This book is intended as a textbook for any college students who are beginning to study language seriously—prospective elementary language-arts teachers, English teachers, linguists, speech teachers and therapists, reading specialists, and students who are "just interested." These people should first learn to think about language on their own and, later, to study what others have written about it. The book may also be used as the text for composition courses.

Though the book is meant to be as unbiased as possible toward any particular linguistic theory, I am sure it is slanted toward structural and transformational grammars, where my training lies. Still, I have tried to invite analysis and evaluation of ideas borrowed from these grammars.

An instructor's manual is available suggesting lines of discussion which it may be useful for teachers to encourage.

Understanding
the structure
of English

introduction

Understanding the structure
of the English language

MAKING GRAMMAR

Making Grammar may strike some people as a strange name for a section of a book. But there is some sense to it. Of course, it all depends on what you mean by *grammar*. There are three common meanings of it going around:

1. The basic *way* a language is put together (In the days of Old English, for example, if you wanted to say that a *glove* had something done to it—"The king threw the glove"—you had to put the root *glof* together with an *-e* ending to make *glofe*.)
2. An *explanation* (or description) of the way language is put together (For example: "Old English nouns of the general feminine declension—*glof*, for instance—have the *-e* ending in the accusative singular.")
3. Some *rules*, many of them questionable, about talking and writing properly ("Don't split infinitives." "Don't end sentences with prepositions." "Use *shall* in the first person, *will* in the second and third." Remember?)

Well, you and I as individuals can't make grammar in the first sense—"the basic way a language is put together." That's been developed by all the speakers of English using language for more than a thousand years, and it's established, already made, except for minor changes going on all the time. And most people are not in-

1

terested in making grammar in the third sense—"some rules, many of them questionable, about talking and writing properly." People may argue about "rules," but they usually don't want to *make* them.

But we can make grammar in the second sense—"an explanation of the way language is put together."

This idea surprises many people at first. They think that explanation of how language is put together was finished years ago and is now complete and available in grammar books. Actually, it isn't so. The way language is put together—its *structure*—remains relatively stable over long periods of time. But the *explanations* of the structure are almost continuously changing; there has never been just one English grammar in this sense—various grammarians or linguists have always held competing theories. And what's more, they haven't described everything there is to describe yet; there are still many things to be explained.

To some extent, then, anybody can make grammar. It's just like having a group of people watch a machine being put together—all of them can describe what they see. Every description will be at least a little different from every other one. And, of course, some will be better than others because they are more accurate in the details of which parts go where and how the parts work together. But, with practice, most people could get pretty good at describing what they observed.

So you can make descriptions and explanations of how language is put together—*make grammar*. So what? Why spend time making grammar? To lead into a discussion of this question, let's first consider a few things about language in general.

SOME THINGS TO THINK ABOUT

1. What's the difference between human beings and other animals? What makes human beings *human?* What does language have to do with being human? Do other animals have language? How does their communication differ from human language?

2. At the age of eighteen months, one of my nephews turned over a brown bag of garbage in the kitchen; and his mother swatted his bottom and chided him: "No, no—don't touch—*garbage!*" For

several weeks, he called an ashtray with cigarette butts in it "garbage"; he also applied the term to his mother's red velvet party dress and to an electrical outlet, among other things. Is it accurate to call his troubles with the word *garbage* an instance of *"language learning"*? Is there more to the process than just "learning a new word"?

3. Below is an excerpt from the transcript of the court-martial of First Lt. William Calley; Prosecutor Capt. Aubrey Daniel III was the interrogator. Can you make a guess as to the relationship between language and thought in Calley's mind in regard to the question under consideration?

DANIEL: What were [your troops] firing at?
CALLEY: At the enemy, sir.
DANIEL: At people?
CALLEY: At the enemy, sir.
DANIEL: They weren't human beings?
CALLEY: Yes, sir.
DANIEL: Were they men?
CALLEY: I don't know, sir. I would imagine they were, sir. . . . I wasn't discriminating.
DANIEL: Did you see women?
CALLEY: I don't know, sir.
DANIEL: Did you see children?
CALLEY: I don't know, sir.
DANIEL: What did you mean, you weren't discriminating?
CALLEY: I wasn't discriminating between individuals in the village, sir. They were all the enemy. They were all to be destroyed, sir.[1]

4. What uses do people make of language? Consider lectures, conversations, greetings, love songs, etc.

5. When you think, do you always think in words? When you use words in your thinking, are they isolated words—or do they occur in sentences? If they occur in sentences, are they sentences like you speak and write?

6. What would the life of human beings be like if they had no language? Imagine the world without language, and for ten min-

---

[1] "Calley's Defense: Anger, Hate, Fear, . . . Orders," *Newsweek*, March 8, 1971, p. 51. Copyright 1971 by Newsweek, Inc. All rights reserved. Reprinted by permission.

utes write whatever comes to mind about the world without language.

7. In *Problems of Art* (1957), Susanne K. Langer makes the following statement:

> Somewhere at the animalian starting line of human evolution lie the beginnings of that supreme instrument of the mind, language. We think of it as a device for communication among the members of a society. But communication is only one, and perhaps not even the first, of its functions. The first thing it does is to break up what William James called the "blooming, buzzing confusion" of sense perception into units and groups, events and chains of events—things and relations, causes and effects. All these patterns are imposed on our experience by language. We think, as we speak, in terms of objects and their relations.
>
> But the process of breaking up our sense experience in this way, making reality conceivable, memorable, sometimes even predictable, is a process of imagination. Primitive conception is imagination. Language and imagination grow up together in a reciprocal tutelage. . . .
>
> . . . Language actually gives form to our sense-experience, grouping our impressions around those things which have names, and fitting sensations to the qualities that have adjectival names, and so on. . . .[2]

Do you agree with Langer about the basic function of language?

LANGUAGE AND PEOPLE

Whatever conclusions you reached from thinking about the questions in the preceding section, you undoubtedly realize that there's something very human about language and something very linguistic about people.

In fact, thinking about how people use language will help you to understand more about what makes people tick than will almost anything else you can do. This statement may at first seem strange —there seems to be so little that's human about many books on language and many courses in English grammar. But that's not the

---

[2] Susanne K. Langer, *Problems of Art* (New York: Charles Scribner's Sons, 1957), pp. 70–71.

fault of language itself; it's just the result of the ways of studying language that some people have used.

Those who stay away from most grammar books and do a lot of looking and listening and thinking of their own will probably get caught up in the fascinating attempt to understand how language works for people. The way that it's put together—its structure—is not all there is to language, but it's a major part, and a part which has much to tell about how the minds of people are put together.

Trying to describe and explain how language is put together—*making grammar*, in the sense I have already explained—is also interesting and important; only after we have a solid description and explanation do we really understand much about how language works.

Now, I can put all this together to form my answer to the question "Why spend time making grammar?" I believe that making grammar is one of the best ways of developing your understanding of one of the most important aspects of human beings—their language behavior.

HOW TO MAKE GRAMMAR

Before we go any further, I'd better show you a little more definitely what I mean by *making grammar*.

Let's take an example from a language other than English—Latin. The six sentences that follow all mean the same thing:

A. Vidit Paulus Mariam.
B. Mariam Paulus vidit.
C. Mariam vidit Paulus.
D. Vidit Mariam Paulus.
E. Paulus Mariam vidit.
F. Paulus vidit Mariam.

Mariam will translate as the English "Mary," *Paulus* as "Paul," and *vidit* as "saw."

How do you know who saw and who was seen?

If you know Latin, you know it's a matter of the endings—*-us* and *-m*. You might begin your analysis of these endings in a very specific way: "The ending *-us* on the word *Paulus* signals that Paul was the one who saw, and the ending *-m* on *Mariam* signals that Mary was the one who was seen."

If you wanted to know more about how Latin in general signals such relationships, you'd look at many other nouns and generalize your account as you found evidence that it should be generalized.

That's *making grammar.*

GETTING STARTED

Before we get down to the business of making English grammar, we need to consider several other ideas.

1. Look at the following sentence:

Agdalikan slokdalikad azdarbu fandkan shandkad.

Can you translate it into English? Of course, not. Why not? Be specific.

I'll tell you something about the meaning of the sentence:

  a. *Agdali*   means "girl."
  b. *Slokdali* means "boy."
  c. *Azdar*   means "choose."
  d. *Fand*   means "tall."
  e. *Shand*   means "short."

Can you translate it yet? ("Girl boy choose tall short"?) What else do you need to know before you can translate it?

Well, here's the rest of it:

  f. The letters *-ka-*, as in *agdalikan*, mean "more than one."
  g. *-n*, as in *agdalikan*, means "one who performs."
  h. *-d*, as at the end of *slokdalikad*, means "one who is affected by action."
  i. *-bu* means "past time."
  j. Descriptive words like *fand* and *shand* have the same endings as the names of the people or things they describe.

With this information, you can translate the sentence as "The tall girls chose the short boys."

Recall the steps you took as we went along:

    k. You started completely unable to understand the sentence.

    l. You got partial understanding when I gave you the meanings of "girl," "boy," "choose," "tall," and "short"—the meanings of the individual base-words.

   m. You got complete meaning when I told you how to find who chose and who was chosen, who was tall, who was short, and when the action took place (in the past)—the relationships among the words.

What does this exercise reveal about the *nature of language?*

2. The language in exercise 1 is an imaginary one—I made it up. Why don't you make up one now? You can do it on your own or with other people. Just follow these rules:

    a. Invent a basic vocabulary of not more than ten words.

    b. Make your invented language work as differently from the way English works as you can imagine.

    c. Make one sentence in your invented language.

After you've done this, write an explanation of how your language works so that anyone can translate your sentence. If you have time in class, it would be interesting to test the clarity and accuracy of your explanation by reproducing it or copying it on the chalkboard to see whether your classmates can translate your sentence by using your explanation. If they can, you're getting good at making grammar.

3. These two exercises show, among other things, that *language is a system.*

Think about the statement that "language is a system"; then write a brief explanation of it.

Why must language be a system for people to use it to communicate?

In light of what we have observed about the nature of language, do you think that the best way to learn a foreign language is to concentrate on vocabulary?

Evaluate the following definition of a *system:*

A system is a group of items organized so that each item has its functions and all items interact as a unit in order to achieve a specific purpose.

Is the English language a system as this sentence defines a *system?*

THE PLAN OF THIS BOOK

The purpose of this book is to help you learn to make grammar. I believe that, by making grammar, you'll come to understand more about how language works in people's minds.

Since many linguists have already written many descriptions of how the English language is put together, it may seem silly to you to try to learn how to make grammar. Why not just study some of the linguists' grammars and let it go at that?

That's fine if it's what you want to do. For one reason or another, however, studying grammar books isn't very useful to most people, and they seldom find it interesting. Trying to figure things out for themselves and trying to explain what they've figured out can be useful in the sense that it's the best way I can think of for really coming to understand how people use language to think, express, establish relationships, and communicate—and understanding *that* should be useful to everybody.

The method of studying language I have described here is much like studying science through doing experiments. It is one thing to read about what scientists have discovered, but quite another to learn what they have discovered through conducting experiments that duplicate the scientists' experiments. Although both approaches are useful, most people learn more effectively through the experiment method—through doing things for themselves.

If you work your way through this book, you will develop what will be in many ways your own analysis of the main features of English structure. We will omit many details of structure, but you will have a general understanding of the system by which speakers of English communicate.

The topics covered will be presented as a series of problems. You will be given sets of examples of English structure (or be asked to collect your own data). You will study the data and describe what you find, and frequently you will be asked to devise theories to explain how something works. Each problem is presented in steps designed to help you notice the significant points you must consider in working the problem. Work is divided into three basic parts: (A) background data, (B) the actual descriptive-explanatory problem itself, and (C) questions relating the problem to people's actual use of language. Some problems will have a fourth part, (D), usually asking you to evaluate what someone else has written about the English language.

Take each step in order; do not read on to the next step until you've finished what you are asked to do at any given step—unless you're stalled; then you might try going to the next step to see whether things clear up. Though some items may be unusually simple, they are included to prevent gaps in thought.

Most of the problems will deal with spoken English. Can you think of any good reasons for this emphasis?

The book contains twenty-six problems. Problems 1–8 introduce the basic aspects of English structure; these parts are very general. Problem 9 is a summary. Problems 10–22 take you back over the same ground of the first nine with exercises which help you to fill in significant details. Problems 23–26 provide analysis of some of the main ideas of people who study language professionally—grammarians.

problem 1

An introduction to the sounds of English

A. BACKGROUND DATA

1. This problem deals with the smallest elements that make up spoken words. A good beginning will be the examination of how we say and hear a real word. When a speaker *says* the word spelled *c-a-t*, for example, how do you know that he is saying *cat* and not *cad?*

2. If you weren't sure about the answer to exercise 1, think about this: is the word *cat* just one indivisible sound, or does it consist of separable sounds?

3. How many sounds does each of the spoken words *cat* and *cad* consist of? If you're not sure, study the pronunciations of the following pairs of words:

    a. cat—bat   d. cad—bad
    b. cat—cot   e. cad—cod
    c. cat—cab   f. cad—cap

How do these examples tell you the number of sounds in *cat* and *cad?*

4. To avoid unnecessary confusion, you should consider something about the spellings of words. Are the actual sounds in the spoken word *cat* the same as the names of the letters which spell them in the written word ("see," "ā," "tea")?

10

This question raises a problem I as an author have in this section: the section is all about *sounds,* but I have to communicate to you about them by means of *marks.* It will help for you to think *sounds*—to pretend that we're "talking" about the English language before it ever had a means of writing.

5. To continue the examination of *sounds,* make three lists of spoken words with *cat* as your cue: (a) all the words which differ from *cat* in only the first sound (for example: *bat*); (b) all the words which differ from *cat* in only the middle sound (*cut*); and (c) all the words which differ from *cat* in only the last sound (*cab*). You may write out your lists, but remember you're concerned with the *sounds in the spoken words,* not with the way they're spelled in the written words.

6. In exercise 5, did you come up with examples like *coot* and *caught?* Do the spellings *o-o* in *coot* and *a-u-g-h* in *caught* stand for a single sound each?

7. For practice in identification of speech sounds, say each of the following items in your most precise pronunciation and decide how many individual sounds each has as you pronounce it:

a. bed_____   k. free_____

b. bid_____   l. fee_____

c. bad_____   m. plot_____

d. booed_____   n. pot_____

e. bud_____   o. pleat_____

f. bide_____   p. please_____

g. bowed_____   q. in_____

h. to_____   r. an_____

i. too_____   s. on_____

j. two_____   t. un_____

8. Spelling often complicates identification of speech sounds. To attack this problem, decide whether each of the pronunciations which corresponds to the italicized letters in the following words is one or two sounds:

a. *th*in_____   e. *ch*eap_____

b. *th*en_____   f. bu*dg*e_____

c. ba*ng*_____   g. mea*s*ure_____

d. *sh*ip_____

9. To persuade yourself that certain sounds are different from one another, it is helpful to make words contrasting in only one sound. See how many different words you can make each having three distinctive sounds, all beginning with the first sound in the spoken word *past* and ending with the last sound in *cat: p ___t.*

10. Now it's time to try to identify the sounds that make up spoken English words. Together, the common full pronunciations of the words printed below contain what students of the language generally agree are the distinctive sounds of English. Say the words aloud as you work through the exercise and identify as many different sounds as you can. It will probably be helpful for you to write out your catalog. A possible form for the entries is: "The first sound in *pat.*"

a. pat	n. thin	aa. bait
b. bat	o. then	bb. bet
c. mat	p. pad	cc. but
d. fat	q. leisure	dd. boot
e. vat	r. lad	ee. boat
f. that	s. zoo	ff. bought
g. sat	t. shoe	gg. pond
h. rat	u. judge	hh. haul
i. gnat	v. yes	ii. putt
j. chat	w. hung	jj. poot
k. cat	x. wet	kk. put
l. gat	y. beet	ll. nut
m. hat	z. bit	

11. To clarify each sound identified in exercise 10, list five other words which contain the sound. Insofar as possible, give examples which show the sound in various positions in words (example: *bird, rib*).

a. the first sound in *pat*	j. the first sound in *gat*
b. the first sound in *bat*	k. the first sound in *hat*
c. the first sound in *mat*	l. the first sound in *thin*
d. the first sound in *fat*	m. the first sound in *then*
e. the first sound in *vat*	n. the first sound in *lad*
f. the first sound in *sat*	o. the first sound in *zoo*
g. the first sound in *rat*	p. the first sound in *shoe*
h. the first sound in *chat*	q. the first sound in *judge*
i. the first sound in *cat*	r. the first sound in *yes*

s. the first sound in *wet*

t. the first sound in *nut*

u. the first sound in *deal*

v. the first sound in *toad*

w. the final sound in *hung*

x. the middle (third) sound in *leisure*

y. the middle sound in *haul*

z. the middle sound in *beet*

aa. the middle sound in *bit*

bb. the middle sound in *bait*

cc. the middle sound in *bet*

dd. the middle sound in *bat*

ee. the middle sound in *but*

ff. the middle sound in *boot*

gg. the middle sound in *boat*

hh. the middle sound in *put*

ii. the second sound in *pond*

12. You can usually distinguish among speech sounds better if you know something about how they are made. Experiment with the sounds you identified in exercises 10 and 11 until you can give a general explanation of how you produce speech sounds. Devise your explanation in terms of the flow of air from your lungs. For example, consider what you do with your tongue, lips, and nasal passages in making the last sound in *bun*.

13. The first twenty-four sounds illustrated in exercise 11 above are produced in a different manner from the last eleven. What basic difference is there in the flow of air between numbers 1 to 24 and between 25 to 35? You can begin your analysis by making the *s*-sound and then the *ah*-sound—you should feel a distinct difference.

14. Actually, there are three other sounds like the last eleven. They are the middle sounds in the following words:

loud   Lloyd   lied

Although these three sounds are more like the last eleven than the first twenty-four, they are also slightly different from the last eleven. In what way? When you say them, can you feel the difference in your mouth?

15. How many speech sounds have you identified for English? Are there any others?

16. You should come to realize something significant about this English system of sounds by comparing it to the systems of other languages. Do all languages use all the same sounds that you've identified in English?

17. To get down to details of item 16, consider this question: have you ever heard a person whose native language is, for example,

Spanish, pronounce the following English words in the manner indicated?

   a. *hit* as if it were *heat*
   b. *slip* as if it were *sleep*
   c. *big* as if it were *beeg*

Can you list other similar examples? Why do you think Spanish-speakers use these "non-English" pronunciations? Have you heard similar pronunciations from speakers of other languages such as French and German?

18. Let's look at this situation from another angle. When you say the words *spore* and *pore*, is the second sound in *spore* exactly like the first sound in *pore?* Try this experiment: hold a lighted match as near your mouth as you dare and say the two words distinctly, *spore* first and *pore* next. What happened when you produced the two so-called *p-* sounds? (If you have trouble making this exercise work, try it with several of your friends.)

19. Actually, the *p-* sound in the pronunciation of *pore* has a little puff of air after it that the *p-* sound in *spore* doesn't have, and this puff may cause the flame of the match to flicker or go out. Now, an interesting fact is that almost all speakers of English consider the two sounds as one sound unless they listen more carefully than usual, as you have just done; but native speakers of some Arabic languages, for example, hear two different sounds. How can you account for this difference?

20. Let's consider the implications of the things we've just examined and exercise your imagination a little at the same time. Suppose that your native language is some language other than English and doesn't have the following three sounds that English has:

   a. the first sound in *pot*
   b. the middle sound in *bad*
   c. the last sound in *hung*

In other words, you don't usually distinguish these sounds from other similar sounds. The first sound in *pot* might, for example, seem the same as the first sound in *boy;* the second sound in *bad* might seem like the second in *bed;* and the last sound in *sung* might seem the same as the last sound in *sun.* Let's further imagine that you're learning English. What problems would you have in understanding English words before you learned to recognize and distinguish these three sounds?

21. At this point, your knowledge of the details of the speech sounds of English may not be complete, but you should have a good idea of the general system of sounds. What is the function of speech sounds in language? How do they enable a listener to tell one word from another, for example? They are often called *distinctive* sounds—what do you suppose the word *distinctive* means in this connection?

B. MAKING GRAMMAR

1. Your study of the exercises we discussed in part A, "Background Data," should have prepared you for this part. You won't use everything you figured out in part A here in part B, but the exercises should have helped you collect the data you need.

2. Devise your own brief description of the system of distinctive sounds which are used in the variety of English you speak. (Don't worry about other people's varieties.) It will probably be useful to write up this account and others that follow and keep them in a notebook for reference and study.

Be sure to include in your description the following items:

a. an explanation of how spoken words are composed of distinctive sounds

b. a catalog of the thirty-eight distinctive sounds of English (with examples from your own variety of English)

c. a general account of how the distinctive sounds are produced

d. an explanation of the communicative function of distinctive sounds (that is, how they enable people to distinguish one word from another in speech).

C. GRAMMAR AND PEOPLE

1. The questions in this section focus on applications of the data you've studied to people's everyday use of language. Begin with a general question: what does all the information in part A have to do with real, everyday talking?

2. How many distinguishable sounds is a baby who cannot yet talk capable of making? How do those born in English-speaking society learn to limit the sounds they use in talking to only the thirty-eight or so distinctive sounds of English? Why do you suppose that by adolescence most people have trouble producing—and even hearing—distinctive sounds which occur in another language but not in their native language?

3. Do children learn the distinctive sounds of English as isolated sounds?

4. No doubt, you have heard some small children say things such as *wun* for *run*, *wide* for *ride*, and *willy* for *really*. Can you give a reasonable explanation of why they substitute the *wuh* for the *ruh*? Can you list other common difficulties children sometimes have with distinctive sounds?

5. Is it very likely that a perfectly normal speaker of English might, under certain conditions but without really trying, say something like "By buther doze whid dadsee will bake by playhouse" for "My mother knows when Nancy will make my playhouse"? If you think it is likely, define the conditions and give an informal explanation of the physiology involved.

6. Write the following sentences on a sheet of paper and give it to fifteen or twenty of your friends, one at a time, and ask them to read the sentences as naturally as possible. When they read them, notice how they pronounce the italicized words. You will probably get quite a bit of variety.

    a. The *police caught* the rapist.
    b. *Aunt Frances ought* to sleep *on* the *cot.*
    c. Strangely enough, the *orange* was *greasy.*
    d. Yelling loudly will make you *hoarse.*
    e. *I* saw a *frog* sitting on a *log.*
    f. Have you ever *taught* a *dog* or a *horse* to do tricks?
    g. The *hog was wallowing* in the *dew.*
    h. My *picture* was in the *newspaper Tuesday* or *Wednesday.*
    i. I *have* an *idea* that *Paul* is *lost* in a *barren* place.
    j. A *bird* flew into the *side* of the *barn.*

In studying your results, consider the following questions:

    a. Did the respondents use a so-called long *o* and heavy accent in the first syllable of *police?*

b. Do the vowels of *caught* and *cot* sound alike or different to you? What about *horse/hoarse, frog/log/dog/hog?*
c. How did the respondents pronounce *dew*—like *doo* or *dyou?* Was *Tuesday toozday* or *tyouzday?*
d. What vowel or vowels occur in *Paul, on, lost,* and the first syllable of *orange—ah, oh,* or *aw?*
e. Was there an "extra" sound —an *r*— at the end of *idea?*
f. What vowel occurred in the first syllable of *barren?*
g. What variety did you find in the vowels in *aunt, wallowing, Wednesday, Frances, was, I, side,* and *barn?*
h. What pronunciation did the respondents use for the *ct* in *picture* and the *th* in *that?*

7. Is there a "standard" pronunciation for most words in the United States? Is there a "correct" pronunciation? What's the difference between "standard" and "correct" pronunciation? What evidence can you cite in support of your answers?

8. Compare the results you got in exercise 5 with the results of other members of your class.

D. EVALUATING GRAMMAR

Part D is an extra this time; some problems won't have it. But it deals with something you need to think about every time—evaluating the explanations you write. In this case, I'll ask you to make an informal evaluation of a description which might have been written as the assignment in part B. I won't give you any specific guidelines to follow at this point. Just read the description, decide what's good about it, what's bad about it, and explain your decisions.

The System of Sounds in My Variety of English

I am a native and resident of the southwestern United States. The words in the variety of English I speak are composed of thirty-eight distinctive sounds, fourteen vowels and twenty-four consonants:

the vowel in *keen, beat, bee* the vowel in *bet, said, head*
the vowel in *hit, pin, lid* the vowel in *ash, pan, rat*
the vowel in *jay, cake, made* the vowel in *but, come, dud*

the vowel in *hop, rot, odd*
the vowel in *tool, food, rude*
the vowel in *put, foot, full*
the vowel in *toad, slow, poke*
the vowel in *law, straw, haul*
the vowel in *mice, fry, bide*
the vowel in *ow, sound, plow*
the vowel in *boy, toil, moist*
the initial consonant in *poor*
the initial consonant in *bit*
the initial consonant in *mug*
the initial consonant in *flag*
the initial consonant in *vine*
the initial consonant in *thin*
the initial consonant in *then*
the initial consonant in *tin*

the initial consonant in *din*
the initial consonant in *set*
the initial consonant in *zoo*
the initial consonant in *not*
the initial consonant in *lot*
the initial consonant in *red*
the initial consonant in *shed*
the initial consonant in *cheap*
the initial consonant in *jaw*
the initial consonant in *yet*
the initial consonant in *kid*
the initial consonant in *gut*
the initial consonant in *wall*
the initial consonant in *hot*
the middle consonant in *leisure*
the final consonant in *sing*

Distinctive sounds are produced by alteration in the flow of air as it moves from the lungs out through either the mouth or the nose. The flow can be narrowed or cut off in a number of ways at a number of places. More severe alteration of the flow of air produces consonants, whereas vowels are relatively open. Some consonants involve stopping the air completely and then releasing it suddenly, as in the production of the consonants in *bob* and *pop*. Other consonants have a friction-sound—*fuzz, shoe, the*. The flow of air may be altered by the lips and tongue.

Distinctive sounds are the means by which we can tell one word from another. We are conditioned to hear them as different one from the other, and so we know that, when someone says *mud*, he's not saying *bud* or *thud*, for example. In this sense, they are the building blocks of language.

problem 2

An introduction to the units of meaning in English

A. BACKGROUND DATA

1. This problem deals with units of speech that have meanings. Do any of the distinctive sounds you identified in problem 1 have meanings of their own? Is the fact that *I* and *oh* are one distinctive sound each and have meanings relevant to the basic function of distinctive sounds? Would you say that distinctive sounds *distinguish* one unit of meaning from another or that they *convey* meanings?

2. What is the *smallest* kind of speech unit that has the function of conveying meaning?

3. Are there meaningful units smaller than words?

4. Do any syllables have meanings? Are *syllable* and *smallest unit of meaning* synonymous? Consider: *alimentary* and *precipice*.

5. To clarify the idea of units of meaning, let's examine a specific word. What does the word *replay* mean? Dumb question: how do you know it doesn't mean the same thing as *play*? What does *re-* as it is used in *replay* mean? Is the meaning of *replay* a combination of the meaning of *re-* and the meaning of *play*?

6. Keeping *replay* in mind, examine the following words. How many units of meaning does each have? (Count only those units that have clear meaning in present-day English.)

a. impure_____   d. prearrange_____
b. playback_____   e. pavement_____
c. kindness_____   f. undo_____

7. It's important to consider how units of meaning in a word are related. Would it be reasonable, for instance, to claim that the meaning of the word *season* consists of the two units of meaning *sea* and *son?* Why or why not?

8. And what about the word *surf*—can it be divided into smaller related units of meaning?

9. Which of the following items can be divided into smaller related units of meaning?

a. re-   f. overturned
b. jumped   g. -ness
c. quick   h. open
d. quickly   i. acceptability
e. assessment   j. -ance

(Note: *ump* has nothing to do with the meaning of *jumped*, and *ass* nothing to do with *assessment*.)

10. For practice, divide each of the following words so as to indicate all the smallest units of modern meaning which combine to make the meaning of the word. Draw slashes between each two units of meaning: re/assess/ment.

a. shipshape   g. employee
b. pitched   h. singer
c. pitches   i. actor
d. baseball   j. contentment
e. recovered   k. victimize
f. action   l. correction

11. Before we go any further, we need to note something about changes that take place when units of meaning are combined. Would you say that *theorize* was formed by the same process by which *victimize* was formed? What happened to the last syllable of *theory* in the process? List three other words which undergo a change similar to that in *theorize*. Do the spellings of words change very often when endings are added?

12. It may clarify the idea of how units of meaning are inter-related within words to think about how the units might have been combined starting from scratch. Using *act* as your base, explain how you think the word *reactivation* was formed step by step. That is, if the units of meaning are *re-*, *act*, *-ive*, *-ate*, and *-ion*, which two were combined first, what was added next, and so forth?

13. Does the following explanation of the process by which *prefabricated* was formed seem reasonable to you? Explain your answer.

Pre was added to *fabric* to form *prefabric*; then *-ate* was added to *prefabric* to form *prefabricate*; and *-d* was added to *prefabricate* to form *prefabricated*.

14. Explain the order in which it seems likely that the units of meaning in each of the following words were put together:

a. undependable
b. unexpressive
c. revitalize
d. postoperative
e. correctional
f. disproportionate
g. unlawful
h. incontestable
i. hopelessness

15. If all the units we've noted so far in this problem have meanings, then these meanings can be defined. Most are easy to define—*dog, hay, fur*. The ones that follow are a bit harder to define. Write a precise definition for each italicized unit of meaning in the following words:

a. actual*ize*
b. play*er*
c. involve*ment*
d. kill*ed*
e. automobile*s*
f. *re*arrange
g. *pre*register
h. assail*ant*

16. At this point, let's turn our attention to some of the differences among units of meaning. How do the italicized units of meaning in the left-hand column below differ.from those in the right-hand column as to their dependence on other units of meaning?

a. *pre*determined
b. develop*ment*
c. beau*tify*
d. cheap*en*
e. sweet*est*
f. *hope*ful
g. green*house*
h. *concept*ualize
i. pre*arrange*ment
j. anti*freeze*

17. There is another important kind of difference among units of meaning. The word *theory* is what you've probably learned to call a noun. When the ending *-ize* is added to it, is the resulting word, *theorize*, a noun also? Does the same result occur when you add *-s* to *automobile*?

18. Keep in mind what you observed in exercise 17. How do the italicized endings in the left-hand column below differ from

those in the right-hand column insofar as the way they affect the functions of the words they're part of? To get into this, identify the usual part of speech of each base-word (*create*, for example) and each derived word (*created*).

a. creat*ed*   f. creat*ive*
b. ugl*ier*   g. ugli*ness*
c. compare*s*   h. compar*able*
d. cheap*er*   i. cheap*en*
e. creepi*est*   j. creepi*ly*

19. Most of the preceding exercises have stressed analysis—taking apart words. This exercise demonstrates composition—putting the parts together. Below are two lists of meaningful units of English. In five minutes, see how many words you can make by combining one unit at a time from the left-hand group with one or more units from the right-hand group. Example: *correct + -ion = correction, correct + -ion + -s = corrections*, and so forth. (Some products will require slight changes in pronunciation and some in spelling if you write down your results.)

correct   -ion
connect   -s
girl   -ness
direct   re-
beauty   pre-
act   -less
truth   -al
sweet   -ize
art   -ify
house   -ful
death   -ate
top   -ive
hate   un-
brief   -ly
appear   dis-
simple   in-

20. Just for practice, divide each of the following words into its related units of meaning by writing out the complete underlying spelling of each unit and putting plus-signs (+) between units. Example: *reactivation = re + act + ive + ate + ion.*

a. freedom
b. preregistration
c. supernatural
d. communistic
e. dullish
f. hopelessness
g. jeopardize

h. preferential
i. ceremonious
j. independent
k. expertise
l. realignments
m. insufferably

B. MAKING GRAMMAR

1. Devise an account of the kinds of minimal units of meaning in English and of how they are combined to make words. In your account, explain the following items:

   a. how each unit of meaning we speak (such as *dog*, *-ness*, and *see*) is composed of distinctive sounds (Please provide examples and explanations.)
   b. the difference in independence between units of meaning like *clear*, *home*, and *walk*, on the one hand, and units like *-ly*, *-er*, *-ed*, and *pre-*, on the other hand (Define *independence* in this connection.)
   c. how the products you get when you add some endings to base-words (*girl* + *-s*) are the same in function as the base-words alone, whereas other endings cause different results (*girl* + *-ish*) (To put it another way, are *girl* and *girls* the same parts of speech? Are *girl* and *girlish* the same parts of speech?)

C. GRAMMAR AND PEOPLE

1. When most speakers of English hear words such as *expertise*, *freedom*, *infiltrate*, *colonize*, *hurriedly*, and *manly*, do you think they hear and understand the words as single units of meaning or as composites of smaller meaningful parts? In diagram form, we might ask the question: do they think "colonize" or "colony + ize," "manly" or "man + ly," for example?

2. How are the following pairs of contrasting sentences related to question 1?

   a. Herkimer's main problem is silly.
      Herkimer's main problem is silliness.

b. Suellen turned beautiful.
   Suellen turned beautifully.

c. Bill is happy.
   Will is happier.

d. Jessica has dancing every evening.
   Jessica has danced every evening.

e. Thornhill pitches well.
   Thornhill pitched well.

3. Consider the following learning problem in statistical terms. A typical college dictionary lists approximately 200 words which are formed by prefixing the unit *pre-* to common verbs like *enroll* and *determine;* but many more verbs and other words so formed are in common use, and we can make up some that we've never heard before—*preburn* or *presmoke*—that are not completely impossible. That means thousands of possibilities. Compare the language-learning task required to master both the underlying verbs (*enroll* and *determine,* for instance) and the derived verbs (*pre-enroll* and *predetermine*) with the task people would have if the two meanings in each case ("to place one's name on a roll" and "to place one's name on a roll before the usual time for doing so," for example) were carried by totally unrelated words, like maybe *enroll* and *bedarfle* (instead of *pre-enroll*).

4. Is the plural ending which most nouns can take always a necessary signal of meaning in sentences where it is used? Consider the following sentence:

Those three boys are after me.

How many times does the sentence signal that the number of boys after "me" is "more than one"? Is the plural ending of the noun *usually* necessary?

5. Observe several children between the ages of one and three as they are learning the minimal meaningful units of English. How many of the meanings do they learn by having someone else give them a precise definition such as "a chair is a piece of furniture which is for sitting in and which has a part that sticks up at the back for you to lean against"? How do they learn the meanings of words like *big, ugly, good,* and *nasty?* Just for the record, how big is big, for example? How much reasoning ability do children need

to learn units of meaning? Do you think that they learn anything else in life that is more complex than the meaningful units of language? Do children give strong indication that learning units of meaning is hard or painful? Do human beings seem to have an inborn predisposition to learn units of meaning in language? Why did you answer as you did?

6. Are the gestures which often accompany speech also "units of meaning"?

problem 3

An introduction
to characteristics of
parts of speech

A. BACKGROUND DATA

1. This problem examines the idea of what we usually call *parts of speech*. Perhaps, like many other people, you have already spent many hours in English courses underlining the nouns once and the verbs twice, distinguishing between adjectives and adverbs, and reciting definitions of the parts of speech. Do you believe that such exercises have anything to do with the English language as people actually use it?

2. Let's try a little nonsense. Does the sentence "The asferbic fintoids have collupitated the belvish hingwaps" make any sense to you? Not much, of course. Yet you do know several things about the sentence. You can answer the following questions about it, for example:

  a. Does the sentence tell about an action? If it does, which word indicates the action?
  b. Who or what is the agent of the action?
  c. Who or what is affected by the action?
  d. Is the action continuing or over at the time of the sentence?
  e. How many fintoids are involved?
  f. What kind of fintoids are involved?
  g. How many hingwaps are involved?
  h. What kind of hingwaps are involved?

3. If you have a traditional background in English grammar, you can probably also answer the following question about the sentence given in exercise 2:

What parts of speech are the words *asferbic, fintoids, collupitated, belvish,* and *hingwaps?*

(If you can't answer it, don't worry—you can still succeed with problem 3. Knowledge of traditional grammar is not necessary here.)

4. The ability of speakers of English to answer the questions in exercises 2 and 3 (if they can) is really amazing: they can make certain identifications about five words that they probably have never seen nor heard before. (I made them up.) Can you account for this ability?

5. Twenty years ago, almost all school children memorized the following definitions or other similar ones; and many still do:

A *noun* is the name of a person, place, or thing.

A *verb* is a word that shows action, being, or state of being.

An *adjective* is a word that modifies a noun or pronoun, describing, pointing out, or limiting.

An *adverb* is a word that modifies a verb, adjective, or another adverb, and tells how, when, where, and sometimes why.

A *pronoun* is a word that takes the place of a noun.

A *preposition* is a word that connects its object to the rest of the sentence.

A *conjunction* is a word that joins words, phrases, and clauses.

An *interjection* is a word that shows strong feeling.

Have you ever wondered whether these definitions make sense? Do they *really define?* Let's experiment with them. Understanding exactly what these "definitions" are worth is important to understanding what parts of speech are.

As far as I'm concerned, a definition of anything should present the information necessary to distinguish the thing from everything else in the world. Of course, I'll be reasonable about the matter of defining by admitting that the ability of a definition to do this depends on the experience of the person who hears or sees it and the situation in which it is used. If, for example, someone asks me, "What's a centipede?" a reply of "That's one crawling on your shoulder" meets the requirements of the moment if there actually

is a centipede crawling on the shoulder of the person I am address-
ing and if the person knows what I mean by all the words in my
definition. However, a more careful definition would be necessary
to enable a person to go out into the wide world on a centipede
hunt and to return with only centipedes.

But let's hunt verbs instead—words which, according to traditional definition, "show action, being, or state of being." According
to this definition *alone*, which words would you call verbs in this
sentence?

A violent murder is being committed in that busy block down the
street.

Would you think I was crazy if I identified the italicized
words below as three of the verbs in the sentence *according to the
given definition?*

A *violent murder* is being committed in that *busy* block down the
street.

Give me a chance—try to justify the identification of these
words as verbs *according to the definition.*

I'll try not to push your tolerance too far, but I have several
other questions.

a. According to the definition of an adjective as a word that
"modifies a noun or pronoun," could the italicized words in the
following sentence be considered adjectives which modify the noun
girl?

That angelic-looking child *has heartlessly killed and dismembered
seven baby rabbits.*

b. Since a preposition "connects its object to the rest of the
sentence" and since *the kitten* is traditionally called the object of
petted in the following sentence, isn't *petted* a preposition?

Bert petted the kitten.

c. And what about interjections? They "show strong feeling."
If I say about a girl of whom I am wildly enamored, "She is *beautiful*—I mean *beautiful!*" are the two uses of the word *beautiful* interjections?

After examining the remaining definitions given (for *noun,
adverb, pronoun,* and *conjunction*) in a similarly critical manner,

write down for later reference your judgment of the validity of the definitions.

6. In exercises 3 and 4, we dealt with the interesting ability of many speakers of English to identify certain nonsense words in sentences as to their part-of-speech classifications. Does this ability have anything to do with knowing the traditional definitions given in exercise 5?

7. The extended treatment in exercises 5 and 6 of the traditional definitions of the parts of speech is not just an attack for the sake of an attack. It is intended to help clear away some troublesome fictions about parts of speech. Now, we can get down to the business of what people must *really* know about parts of speech. If I ask you what part of speech *dask* is, you can't give me a definite answer. Why not? If, however, I put it into sentences, you can:

   a. That dask is very old.
   b. Henry and Serena dask every afternoon at 1:15.
   c. I have lost my dask book.

What makes the difference?

8. It's important to note the *order* of your decisions in regard to the item *dask* in exercise 8. Did you first decide what part of speech it is and then observe where it is placed in the sentence, or did you first observe where it is placed in the sentence and then decide what part of speech it is?

9. Just a bit more nonsense. Decide whether each of the italicized items in the following sentence is a noun or a verb, and list all clues that helped you with each decision. Be sure to note such things as positions in the sentence, apparent endings like -s and -ion, and words like *those* and *won't*: what do such items tell you about parts of speech?

   Those beautiful *snapcoles* in the *rapzoid* won't *finkle* or *jesblam* the *obbentation*.

10. All the work you've done so far in this problem deals with words as parts of speech in sentences. This exercise and the next deal with the question of whether or not it is possible to determine with certainty the parts of speech of any words in isolation. To start easy, what can you say about the parts of speech of *run, man, talk, pig, head, sweet, fly,* and *jump*? Are most words like these as far as recognition of their parts of speech in isolation is concerned?

11. It may seem at first that the word *hurriedly* is always an adverb—it's very likely you've never heard it used otherwise. Experience notwithstanding, I have no trouble thinking that someday I might hear someone say, " 'Hurriedly' is the name of the game." Here *hurriedly* is functioning as a noun. Look at some other words each of which likewise seems at first to be only one part of speech:

a.	*ugly* (adjective)	Ugly is my favorite dog.	(noun)
b.	*carry* (verb)	I bought a new carry-case.	(adjective)
c.	*up* (preposition)	I feel up today.	(adjective)

Admittedly, these are unusual sentences; still, they show that the identifications in isolation will not hold up. Do you think this is true for all words?

12. Another angle on parts of speech: some people claim that you can identify parts of speech on the basis of the interrelationships of the *meanings* in sentences. In regard to the sentence "Pigs love slop," they might say something like this:

> In general, the words *pigs* and.*love* may be used as either nouns or verbs. But, when they are used together, you know that *pigs* must be the noun and *love* the verb because that's the only way it makes sense—*love* doesn't *pig*.

Though this may seem to be a reasonable argument, there's a serious problem if you follow the reasoning out. It should follow from this argument that it will make no difference how you order the words *pigs* and *love*, since meaning will tell us *pigs* is the noun and *love* the verb.

Why, then, is the string "Slop love pigs" meaningless, for all practical purposes?

B. MAKING GRAMMAR

1. The background data indicates that nouns, verbs, adjectives, and adverbs are each marked in sentences by special signals. In this problem, you are given an illustration of each of the main signals that may be used to identify nouns and verbs. Each illustration includes two sentences (or strings of words) which contrast so as to reveal the relevant signal. Each illustration is set up to show

only one signal; as a result, some of the sentences are a little odd, but grammatical, and some strings of words are not even sentences. Study the illustrations; then devise an account of the signals of nouns and an account of the signals of verbs. It will probably be best to write your account.

a. Signals of Nouns (The relevant nouns are italicized.)
  (1) They are diabetic. (*Diabetic* is an adjective.)
      They are *diabetics*.
  (2) They doubt love. (*Doubt* is a verb.)
      They love *doubt*.
  (3) It is good. (*Good* is an adjective.)
      It is *goodness*.
  (4) Mervin is diabetic. (*Diabetic* is an adjective.)
      Mervin is a *diabetic*.
  (5) It is red. (*Red* is an adjective.)
      It is *Red*. (Only in written English, a person's name.)
b. Signals of Verbs (The relevant verbs are italicized.)
  (1) The kindness act work. (This is not a sentence, of course—just an unstructured string of words.)
      The kindness act *works*.
  (2) It is rain. (*Rain* is a noun.)
      It is *raining*.
  (3) City fathers plan. (A possible newspaper headline—but it is ambiguous: did the city perform the action of fathering, or did the city fathers perform the action of planning?)
      City *fathered* plan.
  (4) It has rain in it. (*Rain* is a noun.)
      It has *rained* in it.
  (5) Beauty plan fast. (Just a string of words.)
      Beautify plan fast. (Perhaps a line from a telegram sent by a prospective builder to his architect.)
  (6) Cook face demand. (Nothing again.)
      Cook will *face* demand. (Maybe a newspaper headline.)

2. Adjectives and adverbs also have characteristic signals in sentences. Study the signals illustrated below and then compose an account of them similar in manner to the ones you wrote for nouns and verbs. This part is a little harder than B.1—there are no contrasting sentences to highlight the signals; you have to figure out for yourself what they are.

a. Signals of Adjectives (The relevant adjectives are italicized.)
   (1) *Fanatic* beliefs cause trouble.
   (2) He is *comic*.
   (3) It is *helpless*.
b. Signals of Adverbs (The relevant adverbs are italicized.)
   (1) The man ran very *fast*.
   (2) The man turned *gracefully*.

C. GRAMMAR AND PEOPLE

1. Since many people cannot *name* the traditional parts of speech, the ability to do so obviously has nothing to do with the ability to comprehend English. Another question about parts of speech is not, however, so easy to answer. The names of the parts of speech are simply names for *concepts*; you identified the concepts of "noun," "verb," "adjective," and "adverb" in problem 3, part B. Even though it isn't necessary to know the names, is it necessary to know the concepts to which they refer in order to understand English?

2. Test the following sentences on several six-year-old children who have had no formal study of parts of speech:

a. I know some boys who like to purple.
b. I can play a sing for you.
c. We can girl in the morning.
d. A nicely dog lives next door.
e. That is a very walked cat.

Before you read each sentence to a child, ask: "Does this sound okay?" Then read the sentence. If the child answers *no* to the question, ask him why it doesn't sound okay. If he indicates that the words *purple, sing, girl, nicely,* and *walked,* are used "incorrectly," ask him to say something using each correctly.

3. If any of the six-year-olds you interviewed for exercise 2 objected to *purple, sing, girl, nicely,* and *walked,* but do not know the names *noun, verb, adjective,* and *adverb,* how do you account for their objections? Specifically, what knowledge must they have as a basis for their objections?

4. Consider the following sentences:

a. Alice turned beautiful.
b. Alice turned beautifully.

First work out a short explanation of what each means. Then, explain how you know the difference in meaning between the two sentences. Give specific attention to the question of whether it is necessary to know the *concepts* of "adjective" and "adverb" (not the *names*) to interpret the sentences.

5. If you have come to the conclusion that part of learning to speak English is learning that some words work one way, other words work another way, and so forth, study the question of how speakers learn these word classes and devise an explanation of what you figure out.

D. EVALUATING GRAMMAR

1. The subject of the following essay by Waldo E. Sweet is the same subject you dealt with previously in problem 3—the concepts of parts of speech. It contains two terms you may not be familiar with—*morphology* means "the forms of words," and *distribution* refers to "arrangement of words in sentences." Study it with these two questions in mind:

a. Is Sweet's approach to parts of speech in English more reasonable than the traditional definitions you examined in the background data for problem 3?

b. Is the information Sweet gives an accurate representation of the English language in actual use?

Parts of Speech in English[1]

Waldo E. Sweet

Oddly enough, in the past languages were taught on the assumption that they were fundamentally alike. It was believed that there was a universal grammar which applied to all languages, although it was often noted that language X

---

[1] Waldo E. Sweet, *Latin: A Structural Approach* (Ann Arbor: The University of Michigan Press, 1957), pp. 20–22. Copyright © 1957 by the University of Michigan Press.

was deficient in a certain respect or that language Y seemed to have an extra item or two in its inventory.

Now one important thing that languages do share in common is that they contain meaning. It is possible to take this meaning, analyze it, and give names to the divisions that result. You *can* make a classification of persons, places, and things, and if you wish to call these nouns, that is your privilege. The only trouble with it is that it isn't very consistent and doesn't seem to describe the facts of language as well as the newer approach.

What is a noun in English? Does it have the marker *-tli*, like *Nahuatl?* What is an English verb? Does it end in *-t,* like Latin verbs?

In English, just as in every other language, there are formal markers for such distinctions. If no such markers can be found, then the language lacks this particular feature. Much of the difficulty which students have had with English grammar has arisen from the fact that they were asked to identify things which exist in Latin but are not present in English, since the "universal grammar" to which we referred above was based on Latin. Here then is a description of English, condensed into a single lesson.

Parts of Speech

In English we distinguish five major parts of speech: nouns, verbs, adjectives, adverbs, and a class with many subdivisions called function words. Sometimes morphology clearly indicates the part of speech to which a word belongs, as in *breadth, broaden, broad,* and *broadly.* In many cases, however, it is necessary to see the morphology and *distribution* of an English word before we can determine the form class. *Gardens* is a noun in *The gardens are beautiful this spring* but a verb in *He gardens with great pleasure.* The distribution tells us whether it is noun or verb.

A *noun* in English has the following characteristics:

1. Morphologically it has a distinction between singular and plural (*man/men*) and between the common form and the possessive (*man/man's* and *men/men's*). In most nouns, if we disregard the apostrophe (which corre-

sponds to nothing in the spoken language), the contrast is the same in both instances (*boy/boys*).
2. Distributionally it fits into the frame *The _____ is good or _____ is good.*

There is a small but important subclass of nouns called *pronouns*. In addition to the contrast which nouns have between singular and plural and common case and possessive case, pronouns have a further contrast between subjective and objective case: *I/me, she/her,* etc. Although in general they have the same distribution as nouns they do not take the noun-markers *the* or *a.*

A *verb* in English has the following characteristics:

1. Morphologically it has a distinction between singular and plural of the present tense in the third person (*write/writes*) and between present and past (*write/wrote*).
2. Distributionally it fits into one or more of the following frames:
a. *The man _____s the house.*
b. *The man _____s there.*
c. *The man _____s wise.*

Verbs that fit into the first frame (*see, build,* etc.) are *transitive;* those that fit into the second (*sit, swim,* etc.) are *intransitive;* those that fit into the third (*look, is, seem,* etc.) are *connecting.* Some verbs fit into more than one frame (*run, sink,* etc.).

An *adjective* in English has the following characteristics:

1. Morphologically it has a distinction between the positive form, the comparative form, and the superlative form (*big, bigger, biggest*).
2. Distributionally it fits into both of these frames:
a. *The _____ man arrived.*
b. *The man is _____.*

An *adverb* in English has the following characteristics:

1. Morphologically it has the morpheme *-ly.*
2. Distributionally it fits into the frame *The man fell _____.*

Words which do not qualify morphologically but have the same distribution as one of these four parts of speech

are called by names which have the suffix *-al* or *-ial,* as
adjectival, adverbial. The word *slow* in *Drive slow* (leaving
aside the question of whether it is correct) is an adverbial;
it does not have the morpheme marker *-ly,* but it fits into the
frame *The man fell slow. Slowly,* in *Drive slowly,* is an adverb: it is morphologically marked by the *-ly* and fits into
the frame *The man fell slowly.*

The real complexity of English grammar lies in the residue
of words, called *function words:*

the, a, every, no (noun markers)
may, can, must, should (auxiliaries)
not (negator)
very, more, pretty, rather (qualifiers)
and, or, not, but, rather than (connectives)
for, by, in, from, of (prepositions)
when, why, where, how (interrogators)
because, after, when, although (subordinators)
well, oh, now, why (responders)

The criteria for establishing these classes is distribution.
In *The dog is barking* we could substitute the other noun
markers (*A dog, every dog, no dog*) but not the qualifiers
or any other group.

Bear in mind that every language has its own criteria for
setting up such classes, whether by form or distribution
or by both.

problem 4

An introduction to basic sentence patterns

A. BACKGROUND DATA

1. This problem deals with the basic processes of combining words into sentences. Working problems 1, 2, and 3 should have given you a general but valid idea of how distinctive sounds in English are combined to make meaningful units, how these meaningful units either are words or may be combined to form words, and how key words show group features. If sounds, meaningful units, and words were all English had, how effectively would we be able to communicate with one another?

2. What else is there to English sentences besides words?

3. Let's be specific about it. If I were to state the following information to you, what additional information would you need to understand the situation indicated? What is it *essential* to know?

> A woman whose name is *Suzy* and a man whose name is *Jim* were involved in an action which is referred to as *shooting*.

4. If you were constructing a sentence to denote the situation given in item 3, the words *Suzy, Jim,* and *shot* would correspond to the information I gave you. What would correspond to the additional essential information you indicated that you would need? How would you put together the words *Suzy, Jim,* and *shot* to provide this information?

37

5. The exercise of contrasting how an English sentence works with how a sentence in another language works usually clarifies the essence of English structure. In this connection, I cited, in the introductory section called "How to Make Grammar," the Latin sentence "Mariam Paulus vidit," which corresponds to the English "Paul saw Mary." Another Latin sentence is "Maria Paulum vidit," corresponding to "Mary saw Paul." Point out specifically the difference between the means by which Latin signals the relationships in the two situations and the means by which English signals them.

6. In the section "How to Make Grammar," I also indicated that there are five other acceptable arrangements of the three words in "Mariam Paulus vidit." Are there any acceptable variations for the order of the items in "Paul saw Mary"? Why or why not?

7. Would it make sense to say that, in three-word sentences like "Paul saw Mary," the *position* before the verb and the *position* after the verb have "meaning"? If not, why not? If so, how would you define the meaning?

8. The preceding exercises make it clear that word-order is *generally* important in English. But, *specifically*, how significant is the order of the words in the following sentences?

a. Mildred is your friend.
b. Bixby gave Sixby a sock.
c. The president became my friend.

9. Consider for a minute the kinds of words which are ordered. Using the names *noun, verb, adjective,* and *adverb* as you developed them in problem 3, label each word in the following sentences:

a. People are creatures.
b. People are mean.
c. People die.
d. People build cities.
e. Doctors give patients service.

10. Are the parts of the sentence "Matilda is there" exactly the same as the parts of any of the five sentences in exercise 9? If you find differences, specify what they are.

11. Some of the sentences in exercise 9 seem to be structured alike—a and d, for instance. Below are two similar sentences. Are

the words *men* and *demons* related to each other in a below the same way they are related in b?

    a. Men are demons.
    b. Men hate demons.

If not, how would you explain the difference? Which of the sentences in exercise 9 above is sentence 11.a like? Which is 11.b like?

12. As exercise 11 shows, verbs are very important. Do *die* and other similar verbs usually have nouns after them as do *build* and other verbs like it? Do *give* and other similar verbs usually have two nouns after them as in the sentence "Doctors give patients service"?

13. The examples given so far are much simpler than most sentences we actually use. Examine the following set of sentences, some of which are a bit nearer real language:

    a. People build cities.
    b. Those people build cities.
    c. Those people build magnificent cities.
    d. Those people quickly build magnificent cities.

Are these four sentences put together in *essentially* the same way? Explain your answer.

14. Along the same lines, compare the following sentences to those in exercise 9:

    a. The tall, thin woman is my second wife.
    b. My fifth wife is short and thin.
    c. Many people die every day in car wrecks.
    d. Thoughtless people destroy many forests.
    e. That soloist will sing me a song.

Are 9.a and 14.a essentially alike in the arrangement of parts? What about 9.b and 14.b? 9.c and 14.c? 9.d and 14.d? 9.e and 14.e?

15. How many more additions can you make to 14.a and still retain the central idea of "woman is wife"?

16. Many sentences we encounter every day are even longer than those in exercise 14. Would you say that the following long sentence is put together in essentially the same way that 9.d is put together or in a different way?

With the assistance of computers and fantastically sophisticated engineering equipment, today's construction people can quickly and efficiently design and build unbelievably magnificent and sturdy cities.

17. You may have to do some guessing, but try this question anyway. Does it seem likely that all or most of the sentences of English are put together according to a few basic arrangements? If you think not, explain why not. If you think so, list what you believe are the most common arrangements.

18. What do you think is the purpose of the ways in which words are arranged in English sentences? What does arrangement have to do with communicating a message in a sentence?

B. MAKING GRAMMAR

1. Describe the *basic* patterns identified in part A by which words in English are combined to make sentences.

2. Discuss the role in communication of sentence patterns.

C. GRAMMAR AND PEOPLE

1. Some people who study the language of children claim that when children begin to say words like *ma-ma* and *milk* sometime in the second year, they are really using one-word *sentences*. What do you think about this idea?

2. When slightly older children begin to speak two-word sentences, do any of their sentences reflect any of the arrangements of words in the sentences in exercise 9 of part A? Collect sample sentences from four or five average three-year-olds to support your answer.

3. Think of the human mind as a computer for this exercise. Now, suppose that language operates by a person feeding into his mind-computer certain bits of information, each of which is converted into a language-signal for purposes of communication. A simple model of this idea is shown in the accompanying illustra-

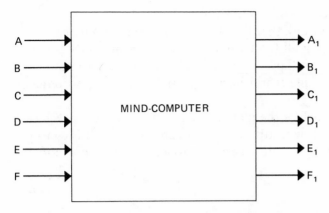

KEY: A, B, C, D, E, F = bits of information;
$A_1, B_1, C_1, D_1, E_1, F_1$ = language-signals.

tion. Next, suppose that a person has the following bits of information, which he feeds into his mind-computer:

A. There is a woman named *Selma.*
B. There is a man named *Vernon.*
C. There is an action called *slapping.*
D. Selma is the agent of the action.
E. Vernon is the recipient of the action.
F. The time of the action is past.

Indicate specifically a language-signal by which each bit of information may be converted into part of a one-sentence statement.

4. Invent several problems more complex than the one in exercise 3 for the mind-computer to process. Indicate and explain the output.

5. Get into a silly frame of mind for a minute. Suppose that the United States Congress enacted into law these two items:

a. Effective immediately, all speakers of English in the United States will replace the word-order of agent-action-recipient (as in "The boys hate carrots") with recipient-action-agent (as in "Carrots hate the boys" meaning that the boys are the agents).
b. Effective immediately, all citizens of the United States will keep their left eyes closed at all times.

Which law would be harder to enforce? Why?

6. Do you think that the children of ancient Rome had more trouble in learning all the Latin endings to put on words as means to indicate relationships in sentences than the children of the modern English-speaking world have in learning the English order of words?

7. How much of the message in a communicative speech situation is conveyed by words in sentences and how much is conveyed by accompanying features—gestures, tone, setting, dress, and the like?

D. EVALUATING GRAMMAR

1. Although problem 4 does not contain an explicit definition of *sentence*, the data you collected in working it is related to the idea of what a sentence is.

2. The short article by Philip S. Dale which follows is an attempt to explain what a sentence is. It contains six technical terms —*morpheme, ordered string, tree diagram, constituent, constituent structure,* and *hierarchical structure*—all of which will be clear in context and none of which you need to memorize. Concentrate, instead, on *how adequately* it explains what you know about English sentences. Specific evaluative questions follow the essay.

Constituent Structure[1]

Philip S. Dale

1)   What is it that makes some utterances grammatical English sentences and some ungrammatical? Before we can answer that question we must look closely at the thing called a "sentence." We can say, "a sentence is made up of smaller units, or words." For example, *I see her* is composed of three words, *I, see,* and *her.* But, many words themselves

[1] Philip S. Dale, *Language Development: Structure and Function* (Hinsdale, Ill.: The Dryden Press, 1972), pp. 7–11. Copyright © 1972 by The Dryden Press. Reprinted by permission of Holt, Rinehart and Winston.

consist of two or more smaller units, each making a contribution to the meaning of the sentence. The word *walked,* for example, consists of two units; *walk,* which is a word referring to a particular kind of action, and the ending *-ed,* which indicates that the action took place in the past. Although the *-ed* ending cannot stand by itself, it is a distinct unit, or element, and can be combined with almost any verb. Similarly, *troubleshooter* consists of three distinct elements, *trouble, shoot,* and *-er,* and the meaning of the word is a composite of the meanings of its three basic elements. These basic elements of meaning are called **morphemes.**

2)   Using the concept of a morpheme, we can now attempt a definition of a sentence: **A sentence is a collection of morphemes.** Some collections are acceptable (that is, they are grammatical sentences) while others are not acceptable (ungrammatical sentences). Now let us compare the sentence *John loves Mary* with *Mary loves John.* They consist of exactly the same morphemes, but their meanings are quite distinct. The difference in meaning is signaled by the difference in **order.**

3)   So now we see that we must take order into account in the definition of a sentence: **a sentence is an ordered string of morphemes.** But, although this is an improvement, it too misses aspects that are important about sentences. Perhaps most important is the way in which sentences seem to break up into **subunits,** or **clusters.** Often a given ordered string of morphemes is **ambiguous,** that is, it corresponds to *two* meanings. For example, *They are eating apples* is ambiguous. One sentence is a statement about some apples; the other is a statement about the activity of several individuals. The two meanings appear to correspond to two ways of breaking up the sentence. In the first, *eating* and *apples* form one unit, and *are* comprises another; in the second, *are* and *eating* form one unit, and *apples* comprises another.

4)   Let's look more closely at this process of dividing sentences. Consider the sentence *The old woman saw a small boy.* (We will return to *They are eating apples* shortly.) The sentence consists of a string of seven words, arranged in a particular order. In addition, the words of the sentence fall into groups, or clusters, which speakers of English have little difficulty in recognizing. Suppose you were asked to

divide this sentence into two parts in the way that seemed most natural to you. Would you produce

> The   old woman saw a small boy

or

> The old woman saw a small   boy

Probably neither; instead you would undoubtedly divide the string into

> the old woman   saw a small boy.

There is something in this string of words which enables you to make this division. If, instead, you were given the string

> brick ham cloud girl dog water tree

which is also an ordered string of seven items, and were asked to divide it naturally, you would have no idea of how to do it. Probably everyone would do it differently. The difference between *The old woman saw a small boy* and *brick ham cloud girl dog water tree* is that the sentence has **structure:** There are natural subunits in the sentence, clusters of words that go together.

5)   One way of indicating how words are clustered in a sentence is to diagram them:

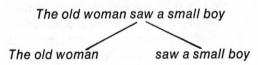

Going further, suppose you were asked to divide the string *saw a small boy* into two clusters. The most likely answer would be *saw* and *a small boy*. The diagram would then look like this:

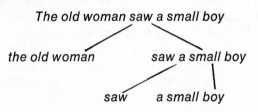

Since diagrams like this begin to look like upside-down trees, minus trunks, they are called **tree diagrams.**
6) The clusters of words into which a sentence can be divided in this way are called the **constituents** of the sentence. We have found four constituents so far: *the old woman, saw a small boy, saw,* and *a small boy.* The example can be continued by dividing *the old woman* into two parts; *the* and *old woman. Old woman* can be divided into *old* and *woman. A small boy* can be divided into *a* and *small boy.* Finally, *small boy* yields *small* and *boy.* Keeping track of all these divisions in a tree diagram produces:

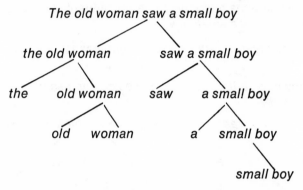

For the sake of completeness, the entire sentence is also considered to be a constituent. Counting it, we have a total of thirteen constituents. Notice that many of the constituents are made up of smaller constituents and, themselves, are part of larger constituents. *A small boy,* for example, is made up of *a* and *small boy* and is part of *saw a small boy.* This kind of structure is called **hierarchical structure.** The fact that language has hierarchical structure is one of its most important properties, for it allows unlimited elaboration of detail to be combined into a coherent structure.

Looking over the thirteen constituents of our sentence, there appear to be some similarities and some differences among them. The constituent *the old woman* seems to be similar to the constituent *a small boy* and *the* seems to be similar to *a,* in a way that is not true of *the* and *small boy.* One way to check if two constituents are of the same general type is to try substitution. To do this, replace each constituent with the other and see if the resulting string of words is a grammatical sentence. For example switching *the* and *small boy,* we have *small boy old woman saw a the* which is not a grammatical sentence. But if we switch *the old woman* and *a small boy,* we have *a small boy saw the old woman,* which is grammatical. In this way we can determine the basic types of constituents.[2]

8)   We have just analyzed the **constituent structure,** that is, the set of constituents and how they are combined, of one sentence. Now let us consider these sentences.

1. My new radio makes an unpleasant noise.
2. The big turkey gobbled his last meal.

These sentences have the same constituent structure as *The old woman saw a small boy:*

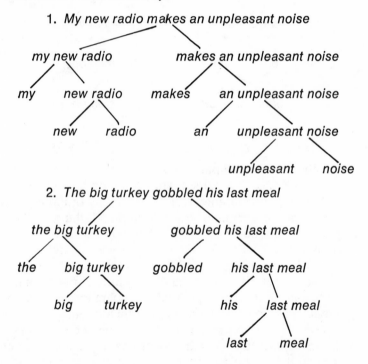

1. *My new radio makes an unpleasant noise*

2. *The big turkey gobbled his last meal*

---

[2] The substitution test is not perfectly reliable, and other techniques must be used in many cases. As an example of the inadequacy of the substitution test, consider the sentences *Falstaff drank hot buttered rum* and *Falstaff drank incessantly* (from R. A. Jacobs and P. S. Rosenbaum, eds., *Readings in English Transformational Grammar,* Xerox, 1970). The constituents *hot buttered rum* and *incessantly* can be substituted for each other in these sentences, but they are not the same type of constituent and cannot be substituted in the frame *I think I'll have another cup of. . . .*

This similarity of structure suggests part of the answer to our question: What makes a string of words a grammatical sentence? The answer is, *if a string of words has a correct English constituent structure, it is a grammatical sentence.* If it violates English constituent structure, it is ungrammatical.

9)   Knowing the constituent structure of a sentence is necessary in order to determine the meaning of the sentence as well as whether or not it is grammatical. Not only must the hearer perceive all the words of the sentence, he must determine the constituent structure to know how the meanings of the individual items are to be combined to form the meanings of the sentence. Now we should be able to understand some kinds of *ambiguity* better. Let us now consider again the sentence *They are eating apples.* The two meanings, one about apples and one about people, correspond to the two constituent structures this sentence can have:

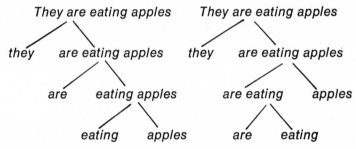

This ambiguity is not due to a difference in words or in the order of words but, rather, to a difference in constituent structure. Another example is the phrase *little girl's bike.* If it is divided (*little girl's*)(*bike*), it refers to a bike which belongs to a little girl. If it is divided (*little*)(*girl's bike*), it refers to a girl's bike that is little.

Evaluative questions about "Constituent Structure"

There are a number of things to think about in the Dale article. The following questions will suggest some of them.

a. What does Dale mean by "grammatical English sentences"? Are speakers of English much concerned with whether or not sentences are grammatical in this sense? Is the kind of grammaticality Dale suggests required for communication through language to take place? (paragraph 1)

b. Is it very likely that the sentence "They are eating apples" would ever really be ambiguous when one person says it to another in a specific situation? If not, what would clarify its meaning? (paragraph 3)

c. Does Dale's analysis treat English sentences as being more nearly independent of actual speaking situations than they really are?

d. Dale asks you to divide the sentence "The old woman saw a small boy" into "two parts in the way that seemed most natural to you." But—in the first place—is dividing the sentence into *two* parts the most "natural" division, or is it just the old drill on subjects and predicates that makes it seem natural? Why not *three*? (paragraph 5)

e. Do you agree with Dale that "knowing the constituent structure of a sentence is necessary in order to determine the meaning of the sentence"? (paragraph 9)

f. Do you think that the ideas in Dale's article might be a reasonable basis for explanations of more complex English sentences?

g. What faults, if any, do you find in Dale's ideas? If you find faults, be sure you can support your claims.

problem 5

An introduction to the basic function of pitch in speech

A. BACKGROUND DATA

1. This problem deals with one aspect of how our voices sound when we say sentences. Through your work in problems 1 to 4, you should have devised for yourself a general theory of how spoken sentences are built from individual sounds. Do you have enough information about how language is put together to explain the means by which you would understand the following sentence if you heard someone say it?

That monster is your enemy.

2. Let's consider the above sentence in a specific context. Assume that you are telling someone who is learning English how to say it and that, at the given moment, he knows the distinctive sounds in the words, the meanings of the words, and the meaning of the arrangement of the words. What else must you tell him before he can say the sentence so that speakers of English will know what he means by it?

3. Imagine that you are trying to teach the person introduced in exercise 2 to say the words "that monster is your enemy" as a *statement* and that, when he says it, his voice goes up on the last word or two, like this:

enemy.

your

That monster is

Is he saying the sentence right?

4. Clearly, how the voice rises and falls is very important in saying sentences. We need to examine it more carefully. Say the following sentence aloud exactly as it is printed, first as a statement, then as a question. What is the distinctive thing that makes the statement a statement and the question a question? How is the highness of your voice used in the distinction?

> My mother is a witch.
> My mother is a witch?

5. Say the following questions aloud in as natural a manner as possible and listen to determine whether the highness and lowness of your voice (the pitch of your voice) goes the same way near the end of each?

> a. Jack has come home?
> b. Nobody believes you?
> c. Are you working?
> d. Is it quitting time?
> e. What did you find?
> f. How old is she?

6. If you didn't find any distinctive difference in pitch among the questions in exercise 5, consider whether it would be possible to say 5.a with the same movement of pitch at the end that statements have? Why? Would it be possible to say 5.e and 5.f with statement pitch? Why?

7. Let's review what we've covered so far about how we use pitch to distinguish between statements and questions in English.

> a. Draw a line the length of the following sentences as printed, beginning just below the first word and going up or down near the end so as to indicate what the pitch of your voice does when you say the sentences:
>
> (1) Mabelle roped the steer.
> (2) Mabelle roped the steer?

b. Through how many levels of pitch must the human voice pass in order to distinguish the question from the statement?

c. Does your voice come down lower at the end of *steer* in the statement than it was at the beginning of *Mabelle?*

8. What would be the effect if your pitch went noticeably higher than usual at the end of the following question?

Jackie has come back?

9. Does your answer to the question in exercise 8 indicate that there is one more level of pitch than you identified in exercise 7?

B. MAKING GRAMMAR

1. Describe as precisely as you can how pitch is used in spoken English to distinguish between statements and questions. Devise, for use in your description, a simple means of picturing the movement of pitch in short sentences when you write them down.

2. In your explanation, show that pitch is an integral part of communicating through spoken language.

C. GRAMMAR AND PEOPLE

1. At some point in their linguistic development, children acquire a concept of "the sentence" in English. I don't mean that they necessarily call it a sentence, but they develop an underlying idea of what the unit we call a sentence is; and, with their knowledge, they can tell when someone hasn't said all of the words he needs to make a sentence. Do you suppose that what you have observed about pitch movement in problem 5 has anything to do with the early stages in children's development of the concept of the sentence?

2. It's sometimes hard to identify just what it is that makes some people who have learned English as a second language sound "foreign" when they speak English. Many who have distinctive sounds, suffixes, and word-order down pat still don't sound like native speakers. Could it be that some of these have trouble with

the pitch movements you studied in parts A and B? If you think so, can you explain why they would have trouble with pitch?

3. Is the pitch discussed in part A relative or absolute pitch?

4. Is there anything unusual about the pitch of people who talk in what seem to you to be "monotonous" voices?

5. The pitch of the human voice dealt with in this problem is a basic element in speech. Do speakers use other devices to clarify ideas, emphasize points, and express emotions when they are talking?

problem 6

An introduction to the basic function of stress in speech

A. BACKGROUND DATA

1. This problem deals further with how we say sentences. There's still one more way the person we imagined in problem 5 (someone learning English as a second language) might go astray in saying the sentence "That monster is your enemy." What is it? If you're not sure, divide the words *monster* and *enemy* into syllables and mark the "accented" or stressed syllable in each.

Now, suppose that your imaginary student placed the strongest accent or stress in each as follows instead of as you marked it:

a. en é my
b. mon stér

How would he sound?

2. Let's try an experiment with stress. Try to say each of the words in the following pairs with the same distinctive sounds but with the strong stress on the first syllable once and on the second syllable the other time:

a. ób ject   ob ject
b. súb ject   sub ject
c. cón trast   con trast
d. cón flict   con flict
e. pró ject   pro ject

53

What difference did it make when you shifted the strong stress? What does this exercise show about the importance of stress in English?

3. Mark the strong stress in each of the following words:

a. deny·   f. recover
b. scenery   g. preparation
c. pollution   h. homely
d. police   i. frantic
e. remember   j. sexual

4. So far, we've dealt directly with strong stresses and implied that other syllables are "weak." Are all weak syllables alike?

5. If I ask you to mark the strong stresses in *alternate* as a verb and *alternate* as a noun, you will probably mark them the same: ál ter nate. If I were to ask you whether the middle syllable of one is just about as "weak" as that of the other, you would probably agree that they are: al tĕr nate. What about the last syllables? Is one just as weak as the other? Isn't the last syllable of the verb stronger than the last syllable of the noun?

6. I have marked the strongest stresses in the following words. Say each word aloud several times and try to decide, among the other syllables in each word, whether any seem to sound a little stronger than others.

a. intelléctual   d. sócialized
b. désignate   e. mílitary
c. educátion

7. The first six background exercises deal with stresses in words. Let's turn to phrases and short sentences. Read the following items aloud.

a. the *mean* boy.
b. I *really* loved her.
c. *The* winner is here.

What, if anything, special did you do when you read *mean* in sentence a., *really* in sentence b., and *the* in sentence c.?

8. Now, read each again—in a natural manner:

a. the mean boy.
b. I really loved her.
c. The winner is here.

How did your second readings differ from your first (in exercise 7)?

9. Does it seem that, in phrases and short sentences, one word gets a stronger stress than the others? If so, where does it come in phrases and short sentences spoken in a natural manner?

10. Comment on the effect on meaning of putting the strongest stress in each of the following sentences first on one word, then on another:

    a. I married a mean man.
    b. Is Ann here?
    c. I like Dale and Sue.

B. MAKING GRAMMAR

1. Compose a brief account of stresses (accents) in English words, phrases, and short sentences. Devise a system for marking the various kinds of stresses in your examples.

2. Provide examples showing how words spelled alike may be differentiated by placement of strong accents.

3. What happens if you misplace strong accents in most words?

4. Show how changing phrase stress from one word to another in a phrase or sentence can affect the emphasis.

C. GRAMMAR AND PEOPLE

1. The pronunciation of *police* as "poh-lease," which is rather common in some areas of the South and Southwest, amuses many people who say "puh-lease." Have you ever heard similar stresses in any of the following words?

    a. recall   d. duress
    b. prefer   e. detain
    c. Arab   f. success

Can you think of other examples?

2. Do words like *the, a, an, and, but, or, in, on, of,* and *by* usually get weak or strong stress in normal conversation? Can you cite some exceptions and suggest circumstances under which they might occur?

3. Have you ever heard anyone say "the apple" as if it were a two-syllable word *thapple?* If you have, can you explain how such a pronunciation comes about? List several other similar cases.

4. How are the two *to*'s ordinarily pronounced in the following sentences?

    a. Henri finally came to.
    b. Henri finally came to see me.

Does the difference have anything to do with the strength of the stresses on these words?

5. Do the following items have rhythm?

    a. Red Rover, Red Rover,
       Let Herman come over.

    b. Way down yonder in the land of cotton,
       Old times there are not forgotten.

    c. Tomorow and tomorrow and tomorrow.

What is rhythm and what does it have to do with stresses?

6. Check several major dictionaries published in the last five years to see how they handle the three degrees of stress in marking the words they list.

problem 7

Expansion of basic sentences

A. BACKGROUND DATA

1. This problem deals with sentences that are more complicated than those in problem 4. There you studied basic arrangements of words in short sentences. Review the grammatical description you wrote for part B of that problem before you go on with this problem. Then think about the following question. If speakers of English were limited to using sentences formed in the manner you described in problem 4—that is, according to five or six basic arrangements, one basic sentence at a time—what effects would this limitation have on the way we talk and on our ability to communicate our ideas accurately?

2. Of course, the ways most sentences are put together are more complex than the ways you described in problem 4. Are the parts of more complex sentences just as systematically arranged as the parts of short, simple ones are?

3. In this exercise, we'll examine the last question in more detail. Study the following sentences and specify how they are similar both in content and structure:

    a. Jeremy built the house.
    b. Jeremy built the house quickly.
    c. Jeremy very quickly built the house.

4. Staying with the comparative process, would you say that the two sentences in each of the following six sets contain the same

57

essential sentence parts? (The first sentence in each of sets a to e is from exercise 4.A.9; the first in f is from 4.A.10. Also note that my question here has nothing to do with the meanings of the sentences.) If you answer *yes*, explain the function of the "extra" words.

- a. People are creatures.
  All people are undoubtedly creatures.
- b. People are mean.
  Many people are uncontrollably mean.
- c. People die.
  Many people die every day.
- d. People build cities.
  Some people build cities well.
- e. Doctors give patients service.
  Most doctors give their patients service.
- f. Matilda is there.
  Matilda is still there on the bench.

5. Now, let's look at several pairs of sentences which are related in different ways. Describe in detail how each second sentence in the sets below differs from the first as far as structure is concerned.

- a. Everybody is somebody.
  Is everybody somebody?
- b. All dogs are hairy.
  Are all dogs hairy?
- c. The time is here.
  Is the time here?

6. To extend the examination of questions, how many different ways can you think of for changing the spoken statement "Petunia Mae is here" into a question? List all your examples.

7. The relationship between questions and statements requires scrutiny. How closely related structurally are the statement and the question in each of the following sets of sentences?

- a. Megathorne is stupid.
  Is Megathorne stupid?
- b. The boy is a student.
  Is the boy a student?

c. Birds sing.
   Do birds sing?
d. Babies make a mess.
   Do babies make a mess?
e. Babies give Felix a headache.
   Do babies give Felix a headache?

8. How far can we go with this idea of variations of a basic sentence? Do you think that it is reasonable to claim that each of the following sentences is, in effect, a structural variation of the basic sentence "Alice Marie killed a pig"? (You may need to spend some time defining the term *structural variation* according to the way you interpret it in doing this exercise. What, for example, is *structure* in general? What features must it show? How do you distinguish a structural variation from a totally different structure?)

a. Did Alice Marie kill a pig?
b. Alice Marie did not kill a pig.
c. Did not Alice Marie kill a pig?
d. Alice Marie didn't kill a pig.
e. Didn't Alice Marie kill a pig?
f. Alice Marie didnt' kill a pig, did she?
g. Alice Marie killed a pig?
h. Alice Marie didn't kill a pig?

9. Let's keep the same basic sentence we used in exercise 8— "Alice Marie killed a pig"—and consider some other related sentences. Do you think that the following sentences should be considered as structural variations of "Alice Marie killed a pig"?

a. A pig was killed by Alice Marie.
b. Alice Marie might have killed a pig.
c. Was a pig killed by Alice Marie?
d. When did Alice Marie kill a pig?
e. Alice Marie was killing a pig.
f. What did Alice Marie kill?
g. Alice Marie did kill a pig.

10. If you decided in exercise 9 that the sentence "A pig was killed by Alice Marie" is a structural variation of the sentence "Alice Marie killed a pig," specify how "Alice Marie killed a pig" is

turned into "A pig was killed by Alice Marie." State your directions so that a person who has never produced a sentence like "A pig was killed by Alice Marie" can get the correct results.

11. All the variations we've dealt with in exercises 1 to 10 involve additions or rearrangements. Another kind of sentence which merits our attention is that from which some part seems to be missing. You probably remember that grammar books used to state that orders like "Clean your room right now!" and "Shut the door!" have *you* as "understood subjects." When people hear such orders, do they really understand *you* as the intended performer of the action?

12. Let's consider more carefully what seems to be missing. Do the following two sentences mean essentially the same thing?

    a. You will clean your room right now!
    b. Clean your room right now!

13. Is it a reasonable theory that the sentence "Clean your room right now!" is produced by deleting *you* and *will* from the sentence "You will clean your room right now"? Would it be just reasonable to use "You must clean your room right now!" as the beginning sentence?

B. MAKING GRAMMAR

1. In problem 4, you described the basic arrangements of words into sentences. The first sentence in each of the following four sets is put together according to such basic arrangements. Explain in detail how each of the other sentences in each set could be derived from the basic sentence. The first step in this assignment is simply describing the differences you observe. Then try to explain how the variations from the basic sentence might be achieved.

    a. *Basic sentence:* Loretta is intelligent.
        (1) Loretta is intelligent?
        (2) Is Loretta intelligent?
        (3) Loretta is intelligent, isn't she?
        (4) Loretta is what?
        (5) Loretta is not wholesome.
    b. *Basic sentence:* Carmelita paints bathtubs.
        (1) Carmelita paints bathtubs?

(2) Does Carmelita paint bathtubs?
(3) Carmelita paints bathtubs, doesn't she?
(4) Carmelita paints what?
(5) Carmelita does not paint bathtubs.
(6) Bathtubs are painted by Carmelita.
c. *Basic sentence:* You will scrub my back.
(1) Scrub my back.
d. *Basic sentence:* Hoagy slapped Samantha.
(1) Hoagy did slap Samantha.

C. GRAMMAR AND PEOPLE

1. Which type of sentence do children learn to use first, sentence a or b below?

a. Bobby slapped David.
b. David was slapped by Bobby.

Do any children ever think that the second sentence means that *David* performed the action of slapping and that *Bobby* got the action?

2. Can you think of any conditions in which arrangements like 1.b would state the speaker's intentions more accurately than some like 1.a would?

3. Have you ever heard a baby babble meaningless noises so that they sound like a question instead of a statement?

4. In response to the statement "The dog can't go with us," an adult might ask "Why can't the dog go with us?" A three-year-old child might, however, ask, "Why the dog can't go with us?" What specifically does the adult do to make such a question as "Why can't the dog go with us?" that the three-year-old hasn't learned to do yet?

5. Speakers of English commonly make questions out of statements by tacking a question on at the end of the statement:

a. I must do that, mustn't I?
b. Felix ought to go, oughtn't he?
c. They are beautiful, aren't they?

When one of my daughters was three, she asked, "I better do it, bettern't I?" Where do you suppose she got such an odd form as *bettern't?*

6. Do you think that the question "Did Johnny have a wreck?" means "Is the statement true that 'Johnny had a wreck' "? Is the second question ("Is the statement true that 'Johnny had a wreck'?") a reasonably good translation of what you would understand if someone were to ask you the first question ("Did Johnny have a wreck?")?

problem 8

Combining basic sentences

A. BACKGROUND DATA

1. This problem treats more complications in sentence structure. We got into some rather difficult operations in problem 7. Still, the complexity of our analyses hasn't begun to approach the complexity of many quite ordinary sentences. Just for the fun of it, can you get started on a reasonable explanation of how the sentence "When the wind picked up, we turned around and headed for the first port we could put into" is put together?

2. Well, regardless of how you did with exercise 1, let's back up a few steps right now. Study the following sentences and specify both how they are different and how they are similar:

    a. Children like dolls.
    b. The children like the dolls.
    c. The children like the dolls because you made them.

3. Sentences like 2.c are more difficult to explain than are sentences a and b. Does it seem reasonable to you to account for the organization of the sentence "The man made the footstool when he was young" by saying that it is composed of two simple sentences "the man made the footstool" and "the man was young" combined in a particular way? Give the reasons for your answer.

63

4. Simple sentences such as we are dealing with may be connected in many ways. Are there any significant differences in the *meanings* of the following three items?

    a. The old man went to market. His wife stayed home.
    b. The old man went to market; his wife stayed home.
    c. The old man went to market, and his wife stayed home.

Would you say that they're just three different versions of the same two simple sentences?

5. Are the following sentences also just variations of the same two simple sentences "the old man went to market" and "his wife stayed home" even though the meanings are slightly different?

    a. The old man went to market although his wife stayed home.
    b. The old man went to market, but his wife stayed home.
    c. The old man went to market while his wife stayed home.
    d. The old man went to market because his wife stayed home.

6. This exercise and exercises 7 and 8 examine the words we use to connect simple sentences such as we have covered so far in this problem. The following two sentences mean approximately the same thing:

    a. Jessica danced, whereas Herkimer sang.
    b. Jessica danced, but Herkimer sang.

What is the general relationship between the idea "Jessica danced" and the idea "Herkimer sang" in both sentences? Which words express the relationship?

7. What happens to sentences 6.a and 6.b if, in each, you move the part after the comma up before the part before the comma, as, for example, "Whereas Herkimer sang . . ."? Are both sentences good sentences regardless of which part comes first?

8. What is the purpose of each of the following words when it comes between two sentences as *whereas* and *but* do in exercise 6?

a. because	h. consequently
b. nevertheless	i. unless
c. although	j. moreover
d. until	k. and
e. when	l. after
f. while	m. though
g. before	n. since

9. There are other kinds of complications in sentence structure than those covered in exercises 1 to 8. How similar do the following two sentences seem to be?

a. The girl is a ballerina.
b. The girl who hit Mark is a ballerina.

10. What does the word *who* in sentence 9.b refer to?

11. Can you think of a way of explaining the means by which the sentence "The girl who hit Mark is a ballerina" is put together that would be clear and sensible to someone who is trying to learn to make sentences like this (someone learning English as a second language, for example)? If you can, write it down and let some of your classmates read it and decide whether they think it's clear and sensible?

12. Is your explanation for exercise 11 anything like the explanation suggested in exercise 3 for the sentence "The man made the footstool when he was young"? If it isn't, do you think it would be possible to explain the sentence "The girl who hit Mark is a ballerina" in a manner similar to that suggested in exercise 3?

13. The relationships sentences like that above (exercises 10–12) signal are worth looking at further. Given the two basic sentences "the girl hit Mark" and "the girl is a ballerina," you might combine them as "The girl is a ballerina, and the girl hit Mark" as well as "The girl who hit Mark is a ballerina." What, if any, difference in meaning is there between the two combinations?

14. How far should we carry this idea of making longer sentences by combining shorter ones? Is it confusing, for example, to claim that the following sentences are all derived by combining the two simple sentences "Nelda tripped John" and "John slapped Melba"?

a. Nelda tripped John, but John slapped Melba.
b. Nelda tripped John because John slapped Melba.
c. Nelda tripped John before John slapped Melba.
d. Nelda tripped John, who slapped Melba.

15. Try sentence-combining from the other side—producing rather than analyzing, that is. Combine the sentences within each of the following sets in as many different ways as possible:

a. Aaron left his home.
   His home was old.

    b. Dearborne did the strip.
       Clarice danced a jig.
       The mansion burned to the ground.

16. To pull your observations together, make a list of the processes covered in this problem which are used in combining sentences.

B. MAKING GRAMMAR

1. Describe the basic methods by which the following sentences and others similar to them are derived:

    a. Velma Lee loves Ralph, but Ralph loves Sybil.
    b. Henrietta left home because Cornball keeps house poorly.
    c. Because Cornball keeps house poorly, Henrietta left home.
    d. The woman who stays home all day misses a lot.

Since, in problem 4, you treated the arrangement of nouns, verbs, adjectives, and adverbs into simple sentences, you may omit such information here. Concentrate, instead, on the *meanings* of the relationships between such units as "Velma Lee loves Ralph" and "Ralph loves Sybil" and the *methods* by which these relationships are indicated in the sentences.

C. GRAMMAR AND PEOPLE

1. At what age do most children begin to utter such sentences as "The dog chased the cat, and the cat chased the rat" and "Mama loves Daddy, and Daddy loves Mama"?
2. What about "I'll see you after you get back" and "I skinned my knee when I fell down"?
3. At what age do children learn to use the word *because* accurately in sentences like "I know it because I saw it" and "The floor got wet because the commode ran over"?
4. Are there any limits to the number of units like "who lives there" and "which I saw" that you can string together in sentences like "The man who lives there in the house which I saw is the same man . . ."?

5. Both of the following sentences are odd. Is one easier to keep up with than the other?

    a. The girl who loves the boy who built the ship which carried the king who rules the country where we live is my friend.

    b. My friend is the girl who loves the boy who built the ship which carried the king who rules the country where we live.

6. Do people use more sentences like the ones in exercise 5 in speaking or in writing? Why?

7. The sentence "Dorabelle won the prize although she nearly missed the deadline because she was ill" is not an unusual type of sentence. What about "Dorabelle won the prize although, because she was ill, she nearly missed the deadline"? Where does the trouble begin with sentences like these?

8. In problem 5, you dealt with how speakers often use variations in the pitch of their voices to distinguish between statements and questions. What do they do at the end of parts like "Samantha is well now" in sentences like "Samantha is well now, but she'll never be herself again" to indicate that there is more to come?

problem 9

Summary of problems 1 to 8

A. BACKGROUND DATA

1. I hope the many details and my questions in problems 1 to 8 haven't caused you to lose sight of the main purpose of devising grammatical descriptions of English—to understand how speakers of English know what sentences mean. Do you think that you have gained understanding of this process through working the problems? If you haven't, why not? If you have, explain what you have gained.

2. In preparation for part B of this problem, review the explanations you wrote for the B-parts of problems 1 to 8. Revise any that need it.

3. What aspects of the way that English is put together have we not dealt with in problems 1 to 8? Make a list of the parts of the system of the English language that we have covered to this point.

B. MAKING GRAMMAR

1. Write an informal but careful account of what a person must know about the English language to understand the following sentence when it is *spoken* in a natural manner:

Dan burned the car which the manufacturers would not repair.

68

In writing your explanation, take into account the following questions:

    a. How does the listener know in terms of distinctive sounds that *Dan* and not *Jan* or *Nan* is the person named? That he *burned*, not *turned*, the car? That it was a *car*, not a *bar*, he burned? That the manufacturers *would* not repair it, instead of *could* not?

    b. How does the listener know the following bits of information:
        (1) That the action is in the past?
        (2) That there was one car?
        (3) What the word *manufacturers* means?
        (4) That there were more *manufacturers* than one?

    c. How does the listener know that the *car* rather than *Dan* was set afire? Consider, for example, the difference between these two sentences:
        (1) Dan burned quickly.
        (2) Dan burned the car quickly.

    d. How does the listener know that *car* is a noun? Does he need this information?

    e. How does the listener know that it is the *car* which the manufacturers would not repair?

    f. How does the listener know that the string of words spoken is a statement rather than a question?

C. GRAMMAR AND PEOPLE

1. Can you *demonstrate* that, to understand the sentence, a person must know all the signals you catalogued in part B of this problem?

2. You should have identified in part B a rather *large number* of signals a person must know, yet a person who knows English well would understand the sentence *instantaneously.* Thus, it is a bit puzzling that someone could put so many signals together so fast. Is there a reasonable explanation?

3. It is clear that the elements of language—distinctive speech sounds, minimal units of meaning, sentence-arrangements, and loudness and highness of voice—are closely interacting parts of the system called *language.* Would it be reasonable to claim, however, that language itself is only one element in a complex system called *communication?*

Getting technical: terminology relevant to problems 1 to 9

This section is just for reference. Though you may not need it much right now, it may be useful in the future.

The concepts you have examined in the first nine problems are much discussed by the linguists in their own vocabulary, which gets fairly technical. Because you have already read some of their discussions and will likely read more at one time or another, I'll get a bit technical here and relate some of their key terms to the ideas you've already considered.

PROBLEM 1. The distinctive speech sounds dealt with here are called *phonemes*. A phoneme is the smallest unit of sound that can distinguish one unit of meaning from another. For example, the words *Sue* and *zoo* rime; the only difference between them is that *Sue* begins with a *sss*-sound and *zoo* with a *zzz*-sound. Thus, the *sss* and the *zzz* are phonemes, for they alone distinguish *Sue* from *zoo* in speech. Each word has two phonemes—the initial ones are different; the final ones, the same.

The study of speech sounds in generally is *phonology*. The study of phonemes in particular is sometimes called *phonemics*. The study of how speech sounds are produced, introduced in A.12, is *articulatory phonetics*. It specifies what movements the speech organs must go through to produce each sound.

Pairs of words like *Sue/zoo* and those cited in A.3 are called *minimal pairs*: they contrast in only one place, a minimal contrast,

70

and thus demonstrate that the two sounds involved are separate phonemes.

A.13 deals with the distinction between *consonant-sounds* and *vowel-sounds*. Generally speaking, consonants require more narrowing than vowels of the passage through which air flows to produce speech sounds; vowels are characterized by a comparatively open flow of air.

The vowel phonemes denoted in A.14 (as in *loud, Lloyd,* and *lied*) are *diphthongs,* phonemes each of which consists of two vowels "blended" within the same syllable.

The two *p*-sounds discussed in A.18 and A.19 (as in *pore* and *spore*) are simply variants of one phoneme and are known as *allophones.* Which one occurs in a particular word depends on other phonemes in the word. All phonemes have such variants, though we are conditioned to ignore the difference.

C.6 deals with *dialects.* A dialect is a distinguishable variety of a language. This exercise deals with only one aspect of *dialect differences*—the phonological.

PROBLEM 2. The minimal units of meaning examined in this problem are called *morphemes,* and the study of them is *morphology.* (The term morphology is also used to refer to the structure of morphemes themselves.)

A.12 to A.14 introduce a process known as *immediate constituent analysis.* It is based on the idea of starting with a whole word and dividing it into two parts and each part into two parts and so on until there are no more divisible parts. It is specified that each product of each cut must be a real unit of meaning. Thus, to divide *undependable* into *undepend + able* would be erroneous in that *undepend* is not a real unit of meaning. The right analysis is, first cut, *un + dependable* and, second cut, *depend + able.* This shows that the two units which immediately compose the meaning of *undependable* (its immediate constituents) are *un-* and *dependable* and that, in turn, the immediate constituents of *dependable* are *depend* and *-able.*

A.16 demonstrates the distinction between *free morphemes* and *bound morphemes.* Free morphemes are those which can occur alone as words (such as, *hope* and *house*), whereas bound do not occur as words but are bound to other morphemes in words (*pre-* and *-ment*).

A.17 to A.18 treat the commonly accepted distinction between *inflectional suffixes* and *derivational suffixes:* the product of a base and an inflectional suffix is the same part of speech as the base alone (*create / created*), but the product of a base and a derivational suffix is a different part of speech from that of the base alone (*create / creative*). Although there are complications with this distinction, it is still useful.

The terms *base* (principal morpheme) and *affix* (*prefix* or *suffix*) are relevant to the exercises in this problem, but must not be equated with free and bound morphemes, respectively, since there are bases which are bound morphemes (*aud*ible / *aud*ience / *aud*ition).

An affix such as *pre-* (C.3) which can be used freely to form new words is said to be a *productive affix*. Others are *-ize* (*theorize, glamorize*), *re-* (*replay, rerun*), and *-ness* (*calmness, loneliness*).

PROBLEM 3. I retain the traditional terms *noun, verb, adjective,* and *adverb* in this problem. In recent years, linguists have referred to these as *word-classes* instead of *parts of speech*. A careful analysis of word-classes has been developed, and it has an extensive technical vocabulary. Since this analysis is not introduced until problem 12, however, the special vocabulary is omitted here.

PROBLEM 4. This problem and problems 7 and 8 deal with sentence-structure, technically known as *syntax*. (The term *syntax* is also used to denote the *study* of sentence-structure.) This problem deals specifically with *basic sentence patterns* (such as "Noun + Action verb + Noun," as in "People build cities," and "Noun + Linking verb + Noun," as in "Mildred is your friend").

A.3 to A.4 introduce the distinction between *lexical meaning* and *grammatical meaning*. Essentially, what words like *Suzy, Jim,* and *shot* refer to individually are lexical meaning; what the arrangement of words signals ("Suzy shot Jim" / "Jim shot Suzy") is grammatical meaning.

A.5 deals with the fact that Latin signals through *inflectional suffixes* (*-m* in *Mariam, -us* in *Paulus*) some grammatical meanings that English signals through *word-order* ("Paul saw Mary").

A.11 focuses on the difference between *linking verbs* (*be, seem, look,* and the like) and *transitive verbs* (*build, give, hit* among others), which signal different relationships between the two essential nouns: "Men are demons" / "Men hate demons."

The noun following the linking verb is traditionally known as the *predicate nominative* (or *predicate noun* or *subjective complement*). Linking verbs are sometimes called *intransitive linking verbs* or *copulative verbs*. In recent years, the verb *be* has, for logical reasons, been considered as a special case and called simply *be* or the *be-verb*; in this case, the term *linking verb* has been used for only the other verbs traditionally classified as linking. An adjective following a linking verb (as in "People are mean") is a *predicate adjective*.

C.3 introduces the concept commonly known as *grammatical encoding*—which, in English, is mainly arranging words into grammatical sentences. In terms of the grammatical meaning defined in the preceding discussion (of problem 4), grammatical encoding provides the structure which denotes the grammatical meaning.

PROBLEM 5. The topic of this problem is *pitch patterns*, the significant heightening and lowering of the human voice in uttering sentences. The treatment here is very general. It is widely agreed that English uses four significant *levels of pitch* in speech, three in normal utterances, a fourth for excited ones. These levels are usually designated by the numbers 1, 2, 3, and 4. Level 2 indicates a normal pitch; level 1, lower; and levels 3 and 4, higher pitch. A pitch pattern is denoted by a string of these numbers, as 231, or 233, or 232.

PROBLEM 6. This problem deals with what is commonly known as *accent* but linguists more frequently call *stress*—the loudness and distinctness of syllables in utterances. Three degrees of stress are usually identified for words, as is illustrated in the contrast in accentuation between *alternate* and *alternate* (A.5): the middle syllables of both words are weak, the first of both are strong, and the last syllable of the noun is also weak; but the last syllable of the verb is clearly between weak and strong.

In phrases and sentences, a fourth degree of stress is found, sometimes called *phrase stress*. For example, when we consider the word *tiny* alone, we observe that the first syllable is strongly stressed and the second weakly stressed; but, if we combine it with *a* and *donation* into the phrase "a tiny donation," the stress pattern is slightly different. The main reason is that a phrase itself has a strong stress, which falls on the strongest syllable of the key word. In this case, the key word is *donation*, and the strongest stress will be on the second syllable (*-na-*). In keeping with this point, linguists introduce a fourth degree of stress and would analyze the stress pattern of the phrase "a tiny donation" in this manner: *a* is weak; *ti-* is secondary; *-ny* is weak; *do-* is tertiary; *-na-* is primary; and *-tion* is weak.

PROBLEM 7. Whereas problem 4 deals with basic sentence patterns, this problem and the next deal with *transformations*—systematic alterations of basic patterns. There are three basic transformational processes: *addition, deletion,* and *rearrangement.* Each of the transformations which are dealt with in this problem has one simple sentence as its base and involves rearrangement of the parts or addition to or deletion from them.

A.5 to A.8 treat aspects of the *question transformation* (or *interrogative transformation*); A.10, of the *passive transformation*; and A.11 to A.13, of the *imperative transformation.*

The questions illustrated in C.5 are called *tag questions:* "I must do that, mustn't I?" "Felix ought to go, oughtn't he?"

PROBLEM 8. In contrast to those covered in problem 7, each of the transformations which are treated here in problem 8 consists of two or more basic sentences. The sentences in A.4 are produced by the *conjoining transformation:* "The old man went to market, and his wife stayed home." "The old man went to market; his wife stayed home." In traditional terminology, this process is known as *coordination.*

Sentences like "The old man went to market because his wife stayed home" (A.5) and those in A.3 and A.9 to A.12 are produced by the *embedding transformations*—inserting one sentence inside another. The traditional name is *subordination.*

PROBLEM 9. This problem deals with the general process of *linguistic decoding.* Recognizing the sounds which comprise spoken words is *phonological decoding;* interpreting the meanings of individual words is *semantic decoding;* construing sentence structure is *grammatical decoding.*

problem 10

An introduction to the nature of the English writing system

A. BACKGROUND DATA

1. In this problem, we will examine the writing system of English. The first nine problems have dealt almost entirely with spoken English. Is speech a reasonable beginning for studying the way the English language is put together? Why or why not?

2. To get started with problem 10, try to explain how spoken English and written English are related.

3. A bit of theorizing may be useful here. Consider for a minute how a spoken language might be given a written form:

    a. There might be a written symbol for each distinctive sound. (For example, an imaginary word consisting of the three sounds *sss*, *uh*, and *zzz* might be written with △ to stand for the *sss*-sound, □ for the *uh*-sound, and ▽ for the *zzz*-sound—thus △□▽.)

    b. There might be a written symbol for each syllable. (∧ might stand for the syllable we spell *pre* in English and > for *named*, and the word we spell *prenamed* would be ∧>.)

    c. There might be a written symbol for each minimal meaningful unit. (The meaningful unit *pre* = \, *name* = —, and *d* = /. Thus, *prenamed* = \—/.)

    d. There might be a written symbol for each word. (Thus, instead of *prenamed*, we might have φ standing for the whole word.)

75

4. Why do you suppose I didn't complete the logical progression in exercise 3 and include the idea of one written symbol for each *sentence?*

5. Does any of the four possibilities listed under exercise 3 above seem very *un*likely as a way of writing a language? Why?

6. Which of the methods listed under exercise 3 does English use?

7. The simplest way of writing a language would be to have one written symbol (and only one) for each distinctive sound of speech—does English use this way?

8. In considering the relationship between letters and sounds, we need to review a point we touched on in problem 1. Are the *names* of the letters of the English alphabet the *sounds* that the letters most commonly stand for? Does the letter called *"ee"* (E, *e,Ɛ,ɛ*) usually stand by itself for the *ee*-sound, for example? Think about the following pairs of words in answering these questions: *pet / Pete   met / mete   step / steep.*

9. The so-called long-*e* sound mentioned above (as in *bee*) has at least nineteen different spellings in English, though several are very rare:

a. *e* as in *me*

b. *ee* as in *meet*

c. *ae* as in *Caesar*

d. *eo* as in *people*

e. *ea* as in beat

f. *e . . . e* as in *Pete*

g. *ei* as in *conceit*

h. *ei . . . e* as in *receive*

i. *oe* as in *amoeba*

j. *ie . . . e* as in *grieve*

k. *i . . . e* as in *elite*

l. *ey* as in *key*

m. *ay* as in *quay* (rimes with *key*)

n. *y* as in *berry* (Last syllable is "long -*e*" for most speakers of English.)

o. *ie* as in *brief*

p. *i* as in *Toni*

q. *ye* as in *Johnnye*

r. *ea . . . e* as in *leave*

s. *ee . . . e* as in *Beene.*

How many can you think of for the so-called long -*a* sound as in *bay?*

10. In this exercise, you're asked to consider spellings for the other sounds of English speech. List as many different spellings for each of the following distinctive sounds as you can. (The long -*a* and long -*e* sounds are included to make the list of sounds complete, but you don't have to give examples for them since they are covered in exercise 9.)

a. the first sound in *pat*
b. the first sound in *bat*
c. the first sound in *mat*
d. the first sound in *fat*
e. the first sound in *vat*
f. the first sound in *sat*
g. the first sound in *rat*
h. the first sound in *chat*
i. the first sound in *cat*
j. the first sound in *gat*
k. the first sound in *hat*
l. the first sound in *thin*
m. the first sound in *then*
n. the first sound in *lad*
o. the first sound in *zoo*
p. the first sound in *shoe*
q. the first sound in *judge*
r. the first sound in *yes*
s. the first sound in *wet*

t. the first sound in *nut*
u. the first sound in *deal*
v. the first sound in *toad*
w. the final sound in *hung*
x. the middle sound in *leisure*
y. the middle sound in *beet*
z. the middle sound in *bit*
aa. the middle sound in *bait*
bb. the middle sound in *bet*
cc. the middle sound in *bat*
dd. the middle sound in *but*
ee. the middle sound in *boot*
ff. the middle sound in *boat*
gg. the middle sound in *haul*
hh. the second sound in *pond*
ii. the middle sound in *put*
jj. the middle sound in *loud*
kk. the middle sound in *Lloyd*
ll. the middle sound in *lied*

11. The list you just made doesn't cover all there is to English spelling. In problems 5 and 6, you observed that a spoken sentence is not just a string of distinctive sounds but a string with a variety of pitches and stresses, both of which are an integral part of the meaning of the sentence as spoken. Review these problems briefly. Does English writing have any way of representing stress and pitch?

12. Give the last question fuller treatment. What connection, if any, do the following marks of punctuation have with the way we *say* English sentences?

a. comma   ,
b. hyphen   -
c. dash   —
d. spaced periods   . . .
e. colon   :
f. semicolon   ;
g. single period   .
h. question mark   ?
i. exclamation mark   !
j. quotation marks   " "
k. underlining   _____ (equivalent of italic type)

13. Another feature of English writing is capitalization. Does it have anything to do with the way we say English sentences? Is it necessary to have both a period (or other terminal punctuation) at the end of one sentence and a capital letter at the beginning of the next?

14. Not all English words are spelled out sound by sound. Study the relationship between the standard written numerals 0, 1, 2, 3, 4, 5, 6, 7, 8, 9 and their pronunciations. Is it convenient to have these symbols?

15. English writing has other symbols like numerals. To what extent does English writing use special symbols like &, *, +, and ° (as in 98.6°)?

16. Still another departure from the basic method of English writing is abbreviations. How are they related to speech?

17. Though it is reasonable to devote most of an examination of the English writing system to the spelling of words and to punctuation and special symbols, there are two other features of the system, both often overlooked by analysts. One has to do with writing the words of sentences. In the three-word spoken sentence "Elaine pinched Rafael," for example, saying *Elaine* first, *pinched* second, and *Rafael* third signals that Elaine is the agent of pinched and Rafael is the recipient. How is this relationship signaled in writing?

18. The other feature concerns arrangement of written (or printed) material on the page. Are all written languages ordered from left to right and top to bottom?

B. MAKING GRAMMAR

1. Write an explanation of *how* English speech is represented by the English writing system. Although you need not catalog every possible written symbol, you should indicate clearly what use English writing makes of the following items:

a. the alphabet
b. punctuation marks
c. capitalization
d. written numerals (0–9)
e. special symbols (as, for example, & and *)
f. abbreviations
g. word-order

C. GRAMMAR AND PEOPLE

1. How can you explain the facts that every normal person in society learns to speak but that at least one-third of the world's population does not write or read? Why are many speakers of English illiterate?

2. Why is English spelling taught in schools for as many years as it is and why do so many people misspell common English words?

3. Does Spanish have a simpler spelling system than English? You might also examine spelling of German, Italian, and Latin. What accounts for simplicity of spelling in some written languages?

4. Is the ability to spell accurately a mark of high intelligence?

5. Look up a copy of the International Phonetic Alphabet in a dictionary or speech textbook and familiarize yourself with how it works. Do you think that using it instead of the present system of English spelling would be an improvement? Would it eliminate misspelling?

6. Near the turn of the century, President Theodore Roosevelt gave his approval to a list of about five hundred "simplified" spellings of common English words. Some examples are: *lite, nite, rite* (for *right*), *tho, thru,* and *thoro*. Are the examples really "simplified" spellings? Most of the five hundred quickly died out. Today, you may occasionally run across *tho* or *thru,* but most "English" teachers would "correct" your spelling if you used them. Why do you suppose that those simplified spellings didn't catch on?

Within the framework

If you have successfully completed the first ten problems, you should now be good at making grammar. You should also have a general but clear and workable idea of how the English language is put together to make it possible for people to communicate by means of it. In effect, you have a kind of *framework*, one mainly of your own making, into which you can place details about the structure of English and, thus, see what parts these details play in communication.

The remaining problems in this book take up some of the significant details of the English language. To make it easier to talk about these details, I use a few of the special grammatical terms I explain in the section called "Getting Technical," which follows problem 9—nothing worth memorizing, though. Now, don't get the idea that I really believe that what has gone before is just a playful approach to studying English and, now that I've got you half-way through the book, I'm really going to get down to business. That's not it at all. Using grammatical terms often makes communication easier in some situations, but they're not indispensable.

There are no two ways about it—the abilities you have been developing in problems 1 to 10 are the really important things you'll get out of making grammar: thinking about how English is put together, explaining what you come up with, figuring out how the way it's put together enables people to understand it, gathering examples to support your interpretations, and evaluating ideas about English on the basis of your own experience. I believe these abilities are important because, as I've mentioned before, I believe that they help us to understand a lot about what human beings are. Language is a major part of human life.

As far as I'm concerned, in fact, these abilities are all that most people ever need. Memorizing somebody else's terminology and definitions and learning this grammar and that grammar and still another grammar are not very useful to many of us.

But let's get on with making grammar. The remaining problems go back and pick up the ideas of the preceding problems where we left off with them and help you to carry your thinking and understanding further. I use the same procedures that I used in the first part of the book: I ask you to study some background data and, then, on the basis of it, to do your own thinking, explaining, and evaluating.

problem 11

An introduction to sound-change in English

A. BACKGROUND DATA

1. Overall, this problem deals with variations in pronunciation. But we must first develop a tool for use in this examination. So—right off—one of the most technical things in this book—a special alphabet for denoting the distinctive sounds (*phonemes*) you dealt with in problem 1. Of what general use might such an alphabet be? I'm introducing it here specifically because I'll need it in this problem and in several that follow.

2. This problem is about spoken, not written English; about sounds, not the way we represent them in writing. But, since I have to communicate with you by means of written English, I need a convenient visual means of indicating to you exactly which distinctive sounds I am referring to. As you already know from problem 10, the regular use of the English alphabet is very inexact—the long -*e* has at least nineteen different spellings, for example.

The method I use in problem 1 is perhaps best in the beginning because it's not technical. Remember?—

    a. the first sound in *pat*
    b. the first sound in *bat*
    c. the first sound in *mat*. . . .

This method gets pretty tedious, though, when I have a lot of sounds to refer to. What I need is one visual symbol for each dis-

82

tinctive sound. If, for example, I told you that I would always use a star ☆ when I meant the vowel-sound in *cat*, then you would always know exactly when I meant that phoneme.

The International Phonetic Alphabet that I asked you to look up in 10.c is such a system for indicating sounds by means of visual symbols. The system I use here is based on it. In cases in which an English sound is usually represented in spelling by one letter of the alphabet, I use that letter in my system. Since the first sound in *pat* is usually spelled with the letter *p*, I use the *p* to stand for it. Likewise with *b*, *m*, and some others. But some sounds do not have such simple spellings—the long *-e*, for example. In these cases, I just use the symbols that many linguists have *arbitrarily* settled on —the long *-e* will be represented by the lower-case letter *i* in this system. In several instances, new symbols are introduced.

But there's really no big problem with this system. When you're looking at a word I've written in it, just check back to the main list to see which distinctive sound is represented by which visual symbol. So that you'll know when I'm referring to a sound or to a spoken word, I'll use a special signal—I'll put a slant-mark before and one after it—/ /—that means, "I'm referring to the distinctive sounds, not to usual spelling."

Incidentally, this system is *not* introduced here to suggest that we ought to begin using it rather than our traditional spelling system. It's just a convenience for me in communicating to you here. And there's no point in memorizing it while you're studying this book unless you do it because you want to or because your class will make special use of it. Here it is:

a. the first distinctive sound in *pat*:   /p/
b. the first distinctive sound in *bat*:   /b/
c. the first distinctive sound in *mat*:   /m/
d. the first distinctive sound in *fat*:   /f/
e. the first distinctive sound in *vat*:   /v/
f. the first distinctive sound in *sat*:   /s/
g. the first distinctive sound in *rat*:   /r/
h. the first distinctive sound in *chat*:   /č/
i. the first distinctive sound in *cat*:   /k/
j. the first distinctive sound in *gat*:   /g/
k. the first distinctive sound in *hat*:   /h/

l. the first distinctive sound in *thin*:   /θ/
m. the first distinctive sound in *then*:   /ð/
n. the first distinctive sound in *lad*:   /l/
o. the first distinctive sound in *zoo*:   /z/
p. the first distinctive sound in *shoe*:   /š/
q. the first distinctive sound in *judge*:   /ǰ/
r. the first distinctive sound in *yes*:   /y/
s. the first distinctive sound in *wet*:   /w/
t. the first distinctive sound in *nut*:   /n/
u. the first distinctive sound in *deal*:   /d/
v. the first distinctive sound in *toad*:   /t/
w. the final distinctive sound in *hung*:   /ŋ/
x. the middle distinctive sound in *leisure*:   /ž/
y. the middle distinctive sound in *tall*:   /ɔ/
z. the middle distinctive sound in *beet*:   /i/
aa. the middle distinctive sound in *bit*:   /ɪ/
bb. the middle distinctive sound in *bait*:   /e/
cc. the middle distinctive sound in *bet*:   /ɛ/
dd. the middle distinctive sound in *bat*:   /æ/
ee. the middle distinctive sound in *but*:   /ə/
ff. the middle distinctive sound in *boat*:   /o/
gg. the middle distinctive sound in *boot*:   /u/
hh. the middle distinctive sound in *pond*:   /a/
ii. the middle distinctive sound in *put*:   /ʊ/
jj. the middle distinctive sound in *loud*:   /au/
kk. the middle distinctive sound in *Lloyd*:   /ɔi/
ll. the middle distinctive sound in *lied*:   /ai/

(The last three sounds are represented by two written symbols because they are technically considered to be what you might call compounds—diphthongs—two vowel-sounds run together. Since this distinction won't be necessary for our work in this problem, don't worry about it.)

Now, let me illustrate the convenience of this system. I can, for instance, tell you that there are, among people I know, three different pronunciations of the word regularly spelled *on*: /ɔn/, /an/, and /on/. Or that some people call my sister, whose name is spelled *Mary*, /meri/ and others call her /mɛri/.

Just for practice in deciphering words I write with this special system, put down the regular English spelling of each of the following words to the right of my special version:

a. /kæt/ _____
b. /dək/ _____
c. /roz/ _____
d. /sɪn/ _____
e. /sɪŋ/ _____
f. /sɪŋk/ _____
g. /θæŋk/ _____
h. /θɪn/ _____
i. /ðɪn/ _____
j. /si/ _____
k. /ši/ _____
l. /ruž/ _____
m. /ǰek/ _____
n. /yæŋk/ _____

o. /čərč/ _____
p. /bɪt/ _____
q. /bɪt/ _____
r. /bet/ _____
s. /bɛt/ _____
t. /bɔt/ _____
u. /bat/ _____
v. /bæt/ _____
w. /bət/ _____
x. /bot/ _____
y. /but/ _____
z. /put/ _____
aa. /put/ _____
bb. /pət/ _____

So that you can check yourself, the answers are printed upside down here:

put (for some *put*).

/pet/ ·qq *;put* /tnd/ ·ee *;tooᵈ* /tnd/ ·z *;tooq* /tnq/ ·ʎ *;toq* /toq/
;ttnq ᴉo *tnq* /teq/ ·ʍ *;tᵈq* /tæq/ ·ʌ *;((/tᵊq/* sɹǝɥʇo '/tᵊq/* ʎes
ǝldoǝd ǝɯos) *tɥᵍnoq* /teq/ ·u *;tɥᵍnoq* /tᵊq/ ·ʇ *;teq* /tᵊq/ ·s *;tᴉeq*
/tǝq/ ·ɹ *;tᴉq* /tᴉq/ ·b *;tǝǝq* ᴉo *tǝq* /tᴉq/ ·d *;ɥɔɹnɥɔ* /ɔɹeɔ/ ·o
;ʞunʎ /ʞɥæʎ/ ·u *;ǝʞɐɾ* /ʞǝɾ/ ·ɯ *;ǝᵍnoɹ* /znɹ/ ·l *;ǝɥs* /ᴉs/ ·ʞ
;ǝǝs ᴉo *ǝǝs* /ᴉs/ ·ɾ *;uǝɥʇ* /uᴉɓ/ ·ᴉ *;uᴉɥʇ* /uᴉθ/ ·ɥ *;(ǝldoǝd ǝɯos*
oʇ *ʞuᴉɥʇ* ᴉo) *ʞuɐɥʇ* /ʞɥæθ/ ·ᵍ *;ʞuᴉs* /ʞɥɪs/ ·ɟ *;ᵍuᴉs* /ɓɪs/ ·ǝ *;uᴉs*
/uᴉs/ ·p *;sʍoɹ* ᴉo *'sǝoɹ* '*ǝsoɹ* /zoɹ/ ·ɔ *;ʞɔnp* /ʞǝp/ ·q *;tɐɔ* /tæʞ/ ·e

3. For this problem, I need the system described in 11.A.2 of representing distinctive sounds to get you to consider how sounds work together in words. The list of sounds you made in problem 1 is the basis of English speech, but it's actually a little too simple to be true. Let me show you what I mean. The word spelled *bat* is pronounced /bæt/. But a word derived from it and spelled *batter* is usually pronounced /bædər/—very few people say /bætər/.

Now, I'm not interested in which pronunciation is "correct"— that's another story. The simple fact is that, for most speakers, the /t/ of /bæt/ becomes a /d/ in /bædər/—and what I'm interested in is why it does. I'll give you the necessary background and let you see whether you can figure it out.

Twenty-nine of the thirty-eight distinctive sounds listed in exercise 2 have in common one thing that's useful for us to note here: speakers' vocal cords vibrate significantly when they produce these sounds. All this means is that the small muscles (vocal cords) in your voice box are set in motion by the air you are sending out of the lungs when you produce these sounds, and the vibrations give something significant to the sounds.

To hear for yourself what this explanation means, say the following pairs of sounds aloud while holding your hands tightly over your ears:

a. /s/ and /z/
b. /f/ and /v/
c. /t/ and /d/

The second sound in each pair is exactly like the first except for one feature—the vocal cords vibrate significantly—so you can hear the vibration when you produce the second sound.

You can also hear the vibration in such sounds as /m/, /ž/, and /ǰ/. The twenty-nine sounds which have this vibration are the following: /b/, /d/, /g/, /v/, /ð/, /z/, /ž/, /ǰ/, /m/, /n/, /ŋ/, /l/, /r/, /y/, /w/, /i/, /ɪ/, /e/, /ɛ/, /æ/, /ə/, /a/, /ʊ/, /u/, /o/, /ɔ/, /ai/, /au/, and /ɔi/.

Now, back to /bæt/ and /bædər/. Let's make a simple diagram of the situation. Let + stand for a sound that has the vibration of the vocal cords and − stand for one that doesn't. /z/ is +, /s/ is −, /v/ is +, /f/ is −. /bæt/ has three sounds, and /bætər/ and /bædər/ five each. If we mark each sound in these words with + or −, they will diagram like this:

a. /bæt/   + + −
b. /bætər/   + + − + +
c. /bædər/   + + + + +

Now, can you answer this question using the diagram: What happens in the pronunciation of /bædər/? Why do you suppose it happens?

4. How frequently does the kind of change you have studied in /bæt/ and /bædər/ occur in English speech? Consider the common pronunciations of the following pairs of words in this connection:

a. dirt—dirty
b. worth—worthy

c. north—northern
d. hit—hitter
e. sit—sitting

How many other examples can you list in five minutes?

5. Other alternations in sounds are more extensive in English than the ones we've already examined; in fact, some are universal under ordinary circumstances. One is found in nouns. It seems very easy to explain to someone learning English as a second language how to make singular nouns like the following plural:

a. cat	d. hat	g. store	j. bump
b. dog	e. head	h. itch	k. bum
c. pig	f. plot	i. jump	l. tree

"Just add an *-s*." "No, let's correct that to an *-s* or an *-e-s*."

But what about the way you *pronounce* the plural forms: *cats, dogs, itches.*

Aren't there *three* plural endings in the spoken versions of these three words, each word with one that's different from the other two? What are the actual sounds? How do you tell which nouns get which endings?

6. Let's not take the last question in exercise 5 lightly. Sort the plurals of the following words into three groups according to whether the spoken forms end in /s/, /z/, or /ɪz/ (or /əz/, or maybe even /ɛz/ for some careful people; count these three variants as one):

a. bee	j. play	s. fellow
b. cap	k. tot	t. cake
c. shoe	l. crow	u. paw
d. bib	m. head	v. frog
e. laugh	n. glove	w. bath
f. lathe	o. pass	x. rouge
g. rash	p. buzz	y. church
h. judge	q. time	z. pan
i. song	r. ball	aa. car

Can you see any *pattern* when you get the words into three lists? For those who want it, here's a clue: do words ending in /b/, /d/, and /m/, for example, ever have /s/ or /ɪz/ for plurals? Do words ending in /p/ and /t/ ever have /z/ or /ɪz/? Do words ending in /č/ and /ǰ/ ever have /s/ or /z/?

7. It's easy enough to explain, on the basis of the vibration of the vocal cords discussed in exercises 3 and 4, the placement of the /s/ and /z/ plural endings. If you don't already recognize the principle involved, work it out using the plus/minus system suggested in exercise 3.

8. On the other hand, the occurrence of /ɪz/ is not explained by the same principle. You can develop an informal explanation, however, by considering *where your tongue is placed* in the production of the six distinctive sounds involved: /s/, /z/, /š/, /ž/, /č/, and /ǰ/.

If words ending in these sounds followed the principle you dealt with in exercise 7, words ending in /s/, /š/, and /č/ would take the /s/ plural, and words ending in /z/, /ž/, and /ǰ/, the /z/ plural. Why?

As a result, the last two sounds in the plural of *pass* /pæs/ would be /ss/; the last two in *buzzes* would be /zz/; and so on. What's the problem with /ss/ and /zz/? With /šs/, /žz/, /čs/, and /ǰz/? Why the extra syllable of the plural ending /ɪz/, then?

9. Do the pronunciations of so-called possessive forms (*Dot's, Dad's,* and *Tess's*) follow the same principles discussed in exercises 7 and 8 above?

10. Although I won't lead you into the mechanics of them, I will mention that many other changes in distinctive sounds occur in speech. As natural as most of these other changes are, they are still not universal in application as are those in exercises 5 to 9. Here are examples of other changes:

a. *Don't* is often pronounced /don/ in "Don't do it."
b. The /t/ is also deleted in /jəs/ in "Just think."
c. *Grandpa* is often /græmpə/ or even /græpə/.
d. The *hand* in *handkerchief* is usually /hæŋ/.
e. The *in* in *income* is sometimes /ɪŋ/.
f. A drive-in grocery named *Seven-Eleven* is often called /sɛm-lɛm/.
g. *Some* in *something* is often /səmp/.
h. Many people call *relevant revelant* and *tragedy tradegy.*
i. *Idea* is *idear* and *wash* is *warsh* to some people.
j. Some people say *acrosst* for *across.*

Have you ever noticed similar occurrences in any of the following words and groups of words?

a. once
b. horseshoe
c. Did you?
d. How do you do?
e. Don't you?
f. Where's it at?

g. warmth
h. grandma
i. length
j. softness
k. children
l. situation

Can you think of other examples?

B. MAKING GRAMMAR

1. To begin this part, say the following verb forms aloud:

a. bop—bopped
b. bob—bobbed
c. pat—patted
d. pad—padded

Note the differences you hear in the endings that indicate past time. The past forms of these verbs are the regular ones in English. Make a longer list of other regular verb forms with the same endings. Don't consider such exceptional forms as *took, shot, sang,* and *did,* which are called irregular.

2. Using your catalog, write an account of the oral pattern for regular past forms in English verbs, including an explanation of your idea of why each of the relevant groups of verbs takes the past form it takes.

C. GRAMMAR AND PEOPLE

1. Elocution manuals, quite popular in days gone by, usually instructed readers to "savor" the sound of every letter in a word. Have you ever tried that? Is it possible?

2. A few reading teachers insist that children use /t/ in the middle of words like *butter, matter,* and *latter.* Is this natural for all speakers of English?

3. How accurate a guide to *actual* pronunciation is English spelling? Is it a good idea for children to "sound out" words as many reading teachers have them do?

4. Is it normal to pronounce the same sound twice in words which have spellings containing double letters, such as *butter, killer, popping,* and *diddle?*

5. Some people argue that pronunciations like /sɛm-lɛm/ for *Seven-Eleven* and /dončə/ for *don't you* are the result of "laziness." Do you agree?

6. Is it necessary to pronounce every possible sound in every word you speak to be "fully" understood?

7. You worked in exercise 11.A.4 with the change from /t/ in /bæt/ to /d/ in /bædər/. As far as communication is concerned, using /bædər/ instead of /bætər/ causes no problems since there is no common form *badder* that might cause confusion. But there are cases where the change makes words that are spelled differently sound exactly alike:

    a. writer—rider
    b. rating—raiding
    c. latter—ladder
    d. bitter—bidder
    e. slighting—sliding

How many others can you list? How often do these identical pronunciations in speech cause confusion? Why?

8. Why do you never hear native speakers of English in normal circumstances use such plural nouns as /kætz/ for *cats,* /dɔgs/ for *dogs,* /pɪgɪz/ for *pigs,* /mæčs/ for *matches,* and /jəjz/ for *judges?*

9. Why do you often hear preschool children use such plural nouns as *mans, oxes, foots,* and *gooses?*

10. Do you think it would be an improvement in the English writing system if each of the plural endings and each of the past endings you have dealt with had a distinctive spelling like *cats, dogz,* and *matchez,* and *popt, bobd, and haunted?*

11. Take fifteen or twenty minutes to review the basic linguistic concepts you have covered in problems 1–11; then, consider this question: what does a child have to know about the English language in order to read it? Is learning which sounds are represented by which letters all there is to learning to read?

Some details of nouns, verbs, adjectives, and adverbs

A. BACKGROUND DATA

1. This problem develops a more detailed analysis of the major parts of speech than does problem 3. Problem 3 deals with parts of speech in general terms. Review what you did there before going on with this problem.

2. Problem 3 deals with the signals that identify nouns, verbs, adjectives, and adverbs in sentences. Problem 12 should help you organize your observations on these parts of speech a little better.

To get started, consider the following sentence which has one blank in it:

The _____ will be here.

Which of the parts of speech you studied in problem 3 usually fills the blank in sentences like the example? List ten examples of this part of speech and try each in the blank.

3. Most of the words which usually fill the blank in the sample sentence in exercise 2 have two basic forms, as, for example, *dog/dogs* and *back/backs*. What are the functions of the two forms?

4. Do the following words have the two forms referred to in exercise 3?

91

a. cat   f. fruit
b. horse   g. ox
c. astronaut   h. pig
d. child   i. doe
e. man   j. filament

5. Will the following words satisfactorily fit the blank in the sample sentence in exercise 2?

a. poor   e. manly   i. hopeful
b. walking   f. good   j. squeamish
c. ugly   g. hitting   k. doing
d. competing   h. hateful   l. dead

6. Do the words listed in exercise 5 have two forms like those in the list in exercise 4, as, for example, *dog/dogs* and *back/backs?*

7. Usually, what part of speech is each of the words in exercise 5?

8. Now, consider the following sentence with two blanks:

The _____ horse is _____.

What is the only part of speech that can satisfactorily fill both blanks?

9. Many of the words which will fill both blanks in the sample sentence in exercise 8 above have three forms:

a. sweet   d. sweeter   g. sweetest
b. ugly   e. uglier   h. ugliest
c. cold   f. colder   i. coldest

What is the function of these three forms?

10. Some longer words use a different method to serve the same three functions. Using the following examples, explain what the different method is:

a. beautiful   d. sensational g. intuitive
b. terrific   e. puzzling   h. stupefying
c. porous   f. natural   i. chaotic

11. Will the following words fill either blank of the sample sentence in exercise 8?

a. head   c. top   e. chopped
b. cleaning   d. cookie   f. house

12. Do any of the words in exercise 11 have three forms like those in exercises 9 and 10, as, for example, *sweet/sweeter/sweetest?*

13. Usually, what part of speech is each of the words in exercise 11?

14. A third sentence with a blank in it for a particular part of speech is:

The woman ran very ————.

What's the part of speech?

15. Most of the words which can fit the blank in the sample sentence in exercise 14 are derived from adjectives, as you may have noted in working problem 3. Describe their derivation as exactly as possible.

16. Are there words that do not follow the derivational pattern you described in exercise 15 that can fill the blank in exercise 14? (That is, words that are not of the form of *quickly* and *slowly?*)

17. Do the words which will fit the blank in exercise 14 have various forms similar to the adjectives in exercise 9, as, for example, *sweet/sweeter/sweetest* and *beautiful/more beautiful/most beautiful?*

18. Each of the three parts of speech you have dealt with so far in this problem has two basic types—those which have characteristic forms and those which will fill the same slots in sentences as those with characteristic forms but do not have the characteristic forms. Do verbs also have two types? You may begin to formulate an answer by comparing *develop*, which is ordinarily only a verb, and *man*, which is originally and mainly a noun but is also used as a verb. Do both have past-tense and present-participial (*-ing*) forms?

B. MAKING GRAMMAR

1. Write as full an account as the data in part A supports of (a) the *characteristic positions* of nouns, verbs, adjectives, and adverbs in sentences and (b) their *characteristic forms*. Include an explanation of those words which do not have characteristic forms but share positions with those which do, as, for example, *poor* does

not have the characteristic singular and plural noun forms (*girl/ girls*) but may fill a noun slot (The *poor* are here).

C. GRAMMAR AND PEOPLE

1. Do you think that children first learn to distinguish among part-of-speech concepts (noun, verb, adjective, and adverb, in particular) on the basis of *where* the relevant words occur in sentences?

2. Should books for beginning readers emphasize signals of parts of speech?

3. In parts A and B of this problem, you noted that words like *rich* and *poor*, which are basically adjectives, may be used as nouns, that verbs may occur as nouns and adjectives, and that nouns may occur as adjectives. How extensive is this "class-shifting" in English? Is it an important process? Why? Is it possible to interpret such uses of *rich* and *poor* as cases where the nouns after them are deleted?

4. In the examples in parts A and B, words in one part of speech are shifted to another without any changes in basic forms. Another process involves putting endings on words to denote a different part of speech from the original. For example, *sing* is basically a verb; *-er* may be attached to the end of *sing* to produce *singer*, a noun. Likewise, *theorize*, almost always a verb, is derived from *theory*, a basic noun; *kindness*, a noun, from *kind*, an adjective; and *hopeless*, an adjective, from *hope*, a noun (*hopeless* meaning "without hope"). List as many endings as you can that will

    a. produce verbs when added to nouns
    b. produce adjectives when added to nouns
    c. produce nouns when added to verbs
    d. produce adjectives when added to verbs
    e. produce nouns when added to adjectives
    f. produce verbs when added to adjectives

5. Do speakers of English very often coin new words by any of the six processes listed in exercise 3?

6. Are there any words which were developed by using a combination of two processes listed in exercise 3? Of three processes? Of four?

7. Have you ever noticed the variety of endings we put on the names of places to make names for the residents of the places?

a. New York*er*   c. Chicago*an*   e. Dallas*ite*
b. Paris*ian*   d. Vietnam*ese*   f. Bengal*i*

Can you think of others? Is there any rime or reason to which endings are used with which place-names?

8. Each of the six terms listed in exercise 6 consists of the complete place-name plus the ending. Some other terms are rather odd:

a. Mexican   c. Floridian   e. Swede
b. Texan   d. Chinese   f. Cypriot

What is odd about each one? Can you think of any likely reasons for these oddities?

9. The following verb forms are traditionally called "present-tense forms": *dance/dances, sing/sings, go/goes.* Do people really use them and the comparable forms of other verbs to denote present *time*—that is, an action going on at the moment when a speaker makes a statement?

Other parts of speech

A. BACKGROUND DATA

1. This problem also deals with parts of speech, but not with those covered in problems 3 and 12. So far, you have treated nouns, verbs, adjectives, and adverbs rather fully and have given very little attention to other kinds of words. What other parts of speech are there?

2. To distinguish some of these "other kinds" a little more exactly, try the following substitution tests. List at least five words that could function as each of the italicized words does in the sentences below. (The meanings will vary slightly from the word given, but the functions will remain the same.)

    a. *The* frog has laryngitis.
    b. Louise boxes *very* fiercely.
    c. The canker *will* go away.
    d. The bomb is *behind* the table.
    e. Winda is ill, *but* Willa went home.
    f. Winda is ill, but *she* completed the job.

3. Most of the kinds of words you listed for exercise 2 are significantly different from nouns, verbs, adjectives, and adverbs. How? Just think—

    a. You should remember from doing problem 12 that nouns have two basic forms (*girl/girls*, for example); verbs have four or

96

five (*play/plays/played/playing,* *begin/begins/began/begun/ beginning*); adjectives, three (*sweet/sweeter/sweetest*); and adverbs, three (*well/better/best*). How many different forms do the words you listed for exercise 2 have?

b. When will the English language get some new nouns, verbs, adjectives, and adverbs? When will there be new words like *the, but, she,* and *behind?*

4. If nouns, verbs, adjectives, and adverbs supply the main *content* of sentences, as many grammarians, with good reason, claim they do, what are the functions of the "other words" we're dealing with in this problem?

5. Now, we'll look at these other parts of speech one at a time. Consider the following sentences, which are roughly synonymous:

a. Jake hooked a whale, but he couldn't pull it in.
b. Jake hooked a whale; however, he couldn't pull it in.
c. Jake hooked a whale, although he couldn't pull it in.

In effect, the words *but, however,* and *although* connect the two parts of each sentence (or the two simple sentences which comprise each big sentence).

Note, however, that:

a. The two parts of example a must stay in the order they're in, and *but* must remain where it is.
b. The two parts of example b must stay in the order they're in, but *however* may be placed at several places within the second part (for example: "he couldn't, *however,* pull it in"/"he couldn't pull it in, *however*").
c. The parts of example c may be reversed ("*Although* he couldn't pull it in, Jake hooked a whale"), but *although* cannot be placed within either part.

List other words that operate as do *but, however,* and *although*—five for each.

6. Do you think that the evidence cited in exercise 5 is sufficient to justify designating three classes or subclasses of words which connect two sentences?

7. Turn your attention here to another class of words. Do you think that words like *will* in the sample sentence "Canker *will* go

away" should be called just plain old verbs like *walk, sing, run, eat,* and *go?* Why did you answer as you did?

8. Would you say that it is reasonable to consider the two occurrences of *can* in the following sentences as two different words? Why?

a. Asa *can* play checkers well.
b. Asa will *can* prunes this fall.

What about "Asa *can can* prunes better than anybody else I know"?

9. What about the "doubles" in these sentences?

a. Hickey *will will* Merv his hairpiece.
b. Inalou *had had* a hard life.
c. You *do do* that well.

10. This exercise covers another class of words. In sentences like "The girl is tall" and "The beautiful girl is tall," would it make sense to call both *the* and *beautiful* adjectives?

11. Along the same lines, do you think that, in sentences like "Herbert runs very quickly," it makes sense to call both *very* and *quickly* adverbs? What about in "The *very* tall boy ran *quickly*"?

12. The next part of speech to be considered is the preposition. Can you write a better definition of a preposition (words like *behind* in the sample sentence 2.d above) than the traditional one that states that "a preposition is a word that connects its object to the rest of the sentence"? Be sure to note the "circularity" of the traditional definition—to find a preposition, first find its object; to find the object of a preposition, first find the preposition. . . .

13. Now, for the fifth and last kind of word to be treated here —the pronoun. Many linguists analyze pronouns as a subdivision of nouns. Does this analysis seem reasonable to you?

14. To particularize your answer to the question in item 13, compare pronouns like *I, you, he,* and *it* (usually termed "personal pronouns") with common nouns like *girl, kitten,* and *flea,* on the one hand, and proper nouns like *Asa* and *Daphne,* on the other. Note similarities and differences in sentence-position, variant forms, and use of helping words (such as *a, the, my*).

B. MAKING GRAMMAR

1. Look over the following group of words:

a. will	e. can	i. do
b. would	f. could	j. did
c. shall	g. may	
d. should	h. might	

Each will fit the blank in the following sentence:

Lobo ———— go away.

2. Write a description of the operation of such words in sentences, covering the following questions:

   a. How do these words differ from verbs like *go* and *walk?*
   b. What position do they take in a verb phrase?
   c. What meaning, if any, do they contribute to sentences?
   d. When a statement ("Julie should go," for example) is transformed into a question by rearrangement of the words, what happens to these words?
   e. Where does *not* go in relationship to these words when a positive statement ("Julie should go") is transformed into a negative statement?

C. GRAMMAR AND PEOPLE

1. I mentioned in A.4 that many grammarians call nouns, verbs, adjectives, and adverbs "content" words. What happens to most English sentences if you take out the "other" words?

2. Collect some newspaper headlines that are ambiguous because of the deletion of "other" words.

3. What is the natural pronunciation of *the?* Under what circumstances is it pronounced like *thee?*

4. Are most of the words like *the, very, will, behind,* and *but* weakly stressed in normal sentences?

5. Have you ever learned in school a distinction in meaning between *may* and *can?* If you have, what is the distinction? Do most people make the distinction in talking?

6. Do most people make a distinction between *shall* and *will?*

7. Should speakers distinguish between *may* and *can* and between *shall* and *will?* Should *writers?*

8. Are the words in the left-hand column below present-tense forms and those in the right-hand column the respective past-tense forms? Are there uses for these words in addition to indicating time?

a. will	would
b. shall	should
c. can	could
d. may	might
e. do/does	did

problem 14

Noun phrases

A. BACKGROUND DATA

1. This problem focuses on constructions which are usually referred to as "noun phrases." The noun positions in the basic arrangements for sentences in problem 4 were filled either by nouns alone (*Suzy, Bixby*) or nouns preceded by only words like *a* and *the*. What limitation would it put on your communication if only such phrases could fill noun-slots in sentences?

2. In everyday use, noun positions in sentences are much more varied than problem 4 suggests. For a start, look at this sentence:

The cats are under the house.

Experiment to see how many other words you can insert one at a time between *the* and *cats* without turning out an ungrammatical or ridiculously involved sentence. Compare results with several classmates.

3. The insertion of words, as in the sample sentence in exercise 2, is not a haphazard process. To explore this idea, arrange the following words to precede *fans* in the sentence "_____ fans are in the storeroom" in the order which seems best to you: *red, the, floor, oscillating, metal, seven, ugly*. Is more than one order possible without producing an ungrammatical unit?

4. If you wanted to add the words *grimey, old,* and *obsolete* to the arrangement you derived in exercise 3, where would they go?

5. Could any of the nine words besides *the* referred to in exercises 3 and 4 (*red, floor, oscillating, metal, seven, ugly, grimey, old, obsolete*) ever precede *the* in the phrase?

6. Could any of the following words be added before *the* in the noun phrase you derived in exercise 3: *four, all, many, unusual, some, none?*

7. The eight words preceding fans in the sentence "All the seven ugly red metal oscillating floor fans are in the storeroom" are traditionally classified as adjectives. All they actually have in common are the facts that they precede the noun *fans* and that they add something to the meaning of *fans*. In other ways, they are different. Experiment with them to determine how they differ in (a) positions in sentences, (b) alternative forms (such as *red/redder/reddest*), and (c) the kinds of meaning they provide.

8. The sources of the words we've been studying are relevant. What parts of speech are *metal* and *floor* usually? *Ugly* and *red?* What part of speech is *oscillating* usually?

9. To this point, we've considered only words preceding the noun. Do adjectives ever follow the nouns they are related to?

10. Can you, for example, insert any descriptive words or larger structures after the word *girl* in the following sentence?

The girl likes the horse.

B. MAKING GRAMMAR

1. Beginning with the basic element of noun phrases—the nouns themselves—describe the kinds of words that may occur in noun phrases and their functions and positions. Somewhere along the way, include your own definition of the term *noun phrase.*

2. Confine your account to examples of the type presented in part A of this problem.

C. GRAMMAR AND PEOPLE

1. When children begin to say two-word sentences, do they use words like *a, an,* and *the* before nouns?

2. Do any of the two-word sentences of small children consist of a noun and an adjective? If so, in what order?

3. Adjectives occur in two main positions in sentences—preceding a noun (as in "The *tall* girl is here") and following certain kinds of verbs ("The girl is *tall*"). Do they have the same function in both positions?

4. How extensively do conversationalists use several adjectives in the first position illustrated in exercise 3 ("the *tall* girl")? What about in the second position ("The girl is *tall*")? Do writers use more adjectives in the first position than speakers do?

5. Someone remarked once that *nouns* and *verbs* are the most important kinds of words in sentences. Do you agree? If English had no adjectives, how would your communication be affected?

6. Student writers are often criticized unfavorably for "overloading" their noun phrases with descriptive words. Is there a "load-limit" for noun phrases?

7. How do you account for the fact that the meanings of words like *nice, great, terrific,* and *wonderful* have become so weak as they are in most uses nowadays?

8. In many Romance languages, the adjective usually follows the noun it is related to as in the Spanish "niña *hermosa.*" Is this an unnatural arrangement of words?

9. Some grammarians suggest that sentences like "The beautiful girl is here," in effect, consist of two basic sentences or propositions—"The girl is beautiful" and "The girl is here," in this case. Does this suggestion seem to represent the ideas that people actually get from such sentences?

10. Some grammarians also explain the derivation of sentences like those mentioned in exercise 9 in something like the following manner:

It begins with two basic sentences, "The girl is beautiful" and "The girl is here." *Who* is substituted for *the girl* in the sentence "The girl is beautiful" and the sentence is inserted after *the girl* in the sentence "The girl is here," producing "The girl who is beautiful is here." Next, *who is* is deleted, leaving "The girl beautiful is here." Finally, *beautiful* is moved in between *the* and *girl* with the result "The beautiful girl is here."

Is this too farfetched for you?

problem 15

Verb phrases

A. BACKGROUND DATA

1. In this problem, we turn our attention to verb phrases, which also are more varied than problem 4 suggests. Let's try adding words one at a time to the verb *sings* in the sentence "Jerome sings." If you add the helping word *may* before the verb, what form must the verb have (as in "Jerome may _____")? If you add just *has*, what will be the form of the verb? If you add *is*?

2. Let's analyze the results you got in exercise 1. You should have got the following forms: "Jerome *may sing*." "Jerome *has sung*." "Jerome *is singing*." Each helper caused the main verb to have a different form. Specify which forms:

With *may* as the only helper, the verb is in the _____ form.
With *has* as the only helper, the verb is in the _____ form.
With *is* as the only helper, the verb is in the _____ form.

3. To make things more interesting, think about what happens if you use two helpers at a time. Let's see. With the same noun (*Jerome*), make a verb phrase using the appropriate forms of *may*, *have*, and *sing*. Then try it with *may*, *be*, and *sing*.

4. What if you use the appropriate forms of *have*, *be*, and *sing*?

104

5. Now, try all three—the appropriate forms of *may, have, be,* and *sing.*

6. Another significant part of verb phrases is the form of the first item. Notice the forms of the first items in the following verb phrases:

    a. She *sings.*
    b. She *sang.*
    c. She *may* sing.
    d. She *might* sing.
    e. She *can* sing.
    f. She *could* sing.
    g. She *has* sung.
    h. She *had* sung.
    i. She *is* singing.
    j. She *was* singing.
    k. She *may* have sung.
    l. She *might* have sung.
    m. She *may* have been singing.
    n. She *might* have been singing.

Apparently, the first item of a verb phrase is always one or the other of two basic forms of a verb or helper—what are the two forms?

7. The verb phrases in exercise 6 are representative, but there are a few variations in the forms of the first items in verb phrases. For example:

    a. She *sings.* / They *sing.*
    b. She *has* sung. / They *have* sung.
    c. She *is* singing. / They *are* singing.
    d. She *was* singing. / They *were* singing.

What feature of sentences controls these variations?

8. Let's turn our attention to the meanings denoted by some of the verb phrases we have examined. In addition to the unit of meaning carried by the main verb (such as the ideas of "singing" or "walking" or "being"), what is the main condition of a sentence that the verb phrase denotes? (To get started, note the difference in meaning between "John is singing" and "John sang.")

9. If you wanted to make a statement about the performance of the action of dancing by a woman named *Jessica* and you wanted to denote that the action is in progress at the time (*present* time)

of your statement, would you say "Jessica is dancing" or "Jessica dances"?

10. Although forms like *dances* and *sings*, *walks*, and *kills* are called "present-tense forms," are they really used to denote *present time?*

11. What forms might you use to denote the future time for the dancing of Jessica?

12. State as specifically as you can the differences in time denoted by the following verb phrases:

    a. Jessica *sang.*
    b. Jessica *has sung.*
    c. Jessica *has been singing.*
    d. Jessica *had sung.*
    e. Jessica *had been singing.*

13. Addition of other words to the verb phrases we have been examining is highly standardized. Indicate where the word *not* should be inserted to negate the verb phrase in each of the following sentences:

    a. Jessica sings.
    b. Jessica is singing.
    c. Jessica sang.
    d. Jessica was singing.
    e. Jessica may sing.
    f. Jessica may be singing.
    g. Jessica may have sung.
    h. Jeessica has sung.
    i. Jessica has been singing.
    j. Jessica may have been singing.

14. In some cases where a word may be inserted into a verb phrase at one point or another, the variants will not mean the same thing. Does the sentence "Jessica may *well* have been singing" mean the same thing as the sentence "Jessica may have been singing *well*"?

15. The most common kind of addition to a verb phrase is that of the adverb derived by suffixing *-ly* to an adjective. What would be the most likely place to add the word *horridly* in the sentences in exercise 13?

B. MAKING GRAMMAR

1. Taking four-word verb phrases like *will have been chasing* as the maximum, write an account of the arrangement and inter-relationship of the parts of verb phrases and of their functions as time-indicators.

2. Confine your account to examples of the kind given in this problem.

C. GRAMMAR AND PEOPLE

1. Look back at the lists of verb phrases in exercises 6, 7, 12, and 13 of part B. They illustrate the wide variety of verb phrases and meanings in the English language, but they don't exhaust the possibilities. In addition, there are such forms as the following:

  a. might be built
  b. might have been built
  c. has been built
  d. had been built
  e. will be built
  f. will have been built
  g. might have been being built
  h. will have been being built

How much use of this variety of verb phrases does the average speaker make in everyday conversation?

2. Do writers tap the variety very extensively?

3. Not all the words in verb phrases get the same degree of emphasis. For example, *have* in the phrase *might have gone* gets fairly weak stress under natural conditions. Could this have anything to do with the fact that some people write *might of gone* instead of *might have gone?* If you're not sure, recall *thapple* ("the apple") in problem 6.

4. The verb phrases in some black-American dialects of English vary significantly from the system you have described in part B of this problem. The black-dialect forms have often been dismissed as "erroneous" or "unsystematic." Study the following black-dialect

forms and decide whether they are in fact unsystematic. To assist you in your analysis, the meanings of the verb forms are given on the left and the common verb forms are on the right.

Meaning	Black-English	Common
The action is habitual, repeated.	they *be passing*	they *pass*
The action is occurring right now.	they *passing*	they *are passing*
The action is past.	they *pass*	they *passed*

problem 16

Noun functions

A. BACKGROUND DATA

1. The topic of this problem is the relationships shown by noun phrases in sentences. The italicized words and phrases in the following sentences are commonly called *objects* to denote that they serve a function which is different from that of the nouns before the verbs ("the subject-nouns"). Would you say that each of the italicized items in the following examples is related to the rest of its sentence as all the others are related to the rest of their sentences?

a. Elaine shot *a pig*.
b. Quonsett has *a headache*.
c. Lana walked *her dog*.
d. Simon flew *a small plane*.
e. It cost *a dime*.
f. Penrod runs *a lemonade stand*.
g. Ina knows *the truth*.
h. I teach *English*.
i. I teach *students*.

2. You may consider some of the italicized items in exercise 1 to have different relations from others. Let's examine the idea more carefully. In the following sentences and many others like them, the first noun (*subject*) is said to name the "performer" or "agent"

of the action denoted by the verb and the second noun (*object*) is the name of the "receiver" or "patient." Now, realistically, who or what performs and who or what receives in the following sentences?

    a. Marigold Mae slapped Petunia Kay.
    b. Christabel suffered a headache.
    c. Lola smelled a rose.
    d. Felix saw a rattlesnake.
    e. Ira knows the truth.
    f. Asa shot the gun.
    g. Asa shot Bert.

3. When you get right down to it, the "objects" in the following sentences have positions and forms in common, but the relations to the rest of the sentences are pretty varied. State as exactly as you can how the referent (that is, what the word refers to in the real world) of each italicized word or phrase in the following sentences is related to the action denoted and to the referent of the other noun (*subject*):

    a. The man chopped *wood*.
    b. Grandpa suffered *a stroke*.
    c. I saw *a unicorn*.
    d. They teach *children*.
    e. Phyllis walked *her skunk*.

Consider, for example, whether "a stroke" really receives anything. And does Phyllis actually perform the action of walking?

4. The analysis is even more interesting when two nouns follow the verb, as in these sentences:

             1   2
    a. The boy wrote *the girl a note*.
           1   2
    b. Caruso sang *Selma a love song*.
           1   2
    c. Jody gave *the girls some pansies*.

How do the functions of the nowns labeled 1 differ from those labeled 2?

5. Do all nouns in the position of *the girl, Selma,* and *the girls* in the sentences in exercise 4 have the same relation to the rest of the sentence? Consider the following sentences:

a. Chet will give *Marty* a package.
b. Chet will paint *Marty* a picture.
c. Chet will play *Marty* a game of tennis.

6. And what about the "subjects" of sentences?

a. *Bert* killed the snake with a gun.
b. *The gun* killed the snake.
c. *Slim* received a gift from Fats.
d. *Fats* gave Slim a gift.
e. *Bridget* is burning the trash.
f. *The trash* is burning.

How is the referent of each subject related to the action denoted by its verb?

7. To conclude, what is the relation shown by the italicized nouns in these sentences?

a. Caldwell ran *a mile*.
b. Caldwell ran *yesterday*.

B. MAKING GRAMMAR

1. Devise a brief account of the kinds of relations shown by nouns (and noun phrases) as illustrated by the sentences in part A of this problem.

C. GRAMMAR AND PEOPLE

1. In connection with the following sentences—

a. I teach students English.
b. I teach students.
c. I teach English.
d. I teach.—

do you think it is reasonable to claim that listeners always understand, whether it is fully stated or not, that "I" teach *something to someone?*

2. Most grammar books give a small list of verbs which can have two objects, verbs such as *give, present, send,* and *offer.* In

actual practice, how limited is the occurrence of two objects as in these sentences? Are there many sentences like the following?

 a. Mike sang *Sarah a song.*
 b. Flint paid *Maureen a compliment.*
 c. I'll play *you a game* of craps.

Can you think of other verbs that may have two objects?

 3. It is very common for people to say things like:

 a. Give me a sip.
 b. Hum me a tune.

Have you ever heard the likes of the following?

 a. Give me it.
 b. Hum me it.

 4. Have you ever heard "Give it me"?

 5. What are common ways of expressing the ideas in exercises 3 and 4?

 6. How can you account for the fact that the sentence "Her I gave a diamond" makes sense whereas "Joan John gave a diamond" does not?

 7. What are the roles of the pigs in these two sentences?

 a. The pig smells terrible.
 b. The pig smells awkwardly.

 8. It wouldn't surprise you at all for someone to say "That chicken eats well," meaning the chicken has a good appetite. But what if someone said "That chicken eats well," meaning the chicken as food tastes good?

Complexity in sentence structure

A. BACKGROUND DATA

1. This problem deals with an aspect of constructing longer sentences which we have not dealt with previously. Before you get further into this problem, review parts A and B of problem 8.

2. I suggest in problem 8 the possibility of considering sentences like "The man made the footstool when he was old" and "The girl who hit Mark is a ballerina" each as a combination of two simple sentences. Would it be reasonable to analyze the sentence "We soon realized that Marvin was a screwball" as being likewise a combination of two simple sentences?

3. How is the structure of the sentence "We soon realized that Marvin was a screwball" different from that of "The man made the footstool when he was old" and "The girl who hit Mark is a ballerina"?

4. Combinations such as we are examining here are not achieved by just slapping two simple sentences together. To get to the bottom of the matter, let's start with a simple exercise. Combine the two sentences "Louise knows something" and "Ferdinand is a transvestite" so that the sentence "Ferdinand is a transvestite" replaces the word *something* in the sentence "Louise knows something." Does the word *that* have to precede the sentence "Ferdinand is a transvestite"?

113

5. Next, combine "Porgy requested something" and "Bess wears a wig" in a manner similar to that outlined in exercise 4. What changes are necessary here that were not necessary in exercise 4?

6. Label the parts of speech for the italicized words in this sentence:

Porgy requested that *Bess wear a wig*.

Now, compare the sentence "Porgy requested Bess to wear a wig" to the sentence "Porgy requested that Bess wear a wig." What's similar about them? What's different?

7. The string of words "Bess wear a wig" is clearly constructed according to one of the sentence-patterns covered in problem 4. Which one? Does it seem reasonable to consider that the string of words "Bess to wear a wig" is also constructed according to one of these patterns? Explain why you answered as you did.

8. Such alternative forms get even more complicated in some cases. Combine the sentences "Something seems strange" and "She is gone" as you combined the two sentences in exercises 4 and 5. This is fairly simple. If, on the other hand, you want to substitute "her to be gone" for *something* in "Something seems strange," what change must you make?

9. In exercise 7, you explored the possibility of considering "Bess to wear a wig" in "Porgy requested Bess to wear a wig" as an altered version of a basic sentence. What about "to wear a wig" in "Porgy wanted to wear a wig"? Is it also a variation of a basic sentence?

10. Or consider this case. Is "Mary Helen's murdering her father" in the sentence "Mary Helen's murdering her father is unbelievable" equivalent to "That Mary Helen murdered her father" in the sentence "That Mary Helen murdered her father is unbelievable"? Does the string "Mary Helen's murdering her father" have a subject-noun, a verb, and an object-noun just as "Mary Helen murdered her father" does?

11. Just how far can compression of sentence-parts be carried? For example, would you say that the italicized parts of the following sentences are themselves abbreviated basic sentences?

a. Some vegetarians marry *beef-eaters*.
b. *The fast talker* sometimes fools people.

c. Hawthorne is a *n'er-do-well*.
d. Caruso was a better *actor* than *singer*.

B. MAKING GRAMMAR

1. For your grammatical description here, assume that the sentence "The well having gone dry, we hired a rain-dancer" is composed of two simple sentences based on the following patterns:

Noun + Verb + Adjective
Subject-noun + Verb + Object-noun

More specifically, the underlying sentences would be something like this:

a. Noun +   Verb   + Adjective
   the well + some form of *have* + *gone* + *dry*

b. Subject-noun + Verb + Object-noun
   we   + *hired* + *a rain-dancer.*

2. Now, write exact instructions for turning these underlying sentences into the actual sentence "The well having gone dry, we hired a rain-dancer." The instructions need not be more than a sentence or two long.

So you won't feel cheated, however, also write a specific explanation of how the two basic sentences are related in meaning in the final product (that is, "The well having gone dry, we hired a rain-dancer").

C. GRAMMAR AND PEOPLE

1. Are sentences structured like "The well having gone dry, we hired a rain-dancer" very common in everyday conversation? Would you say that they are of a "literary style"? How would you most likely state the idea of this sentence in talking?

2. In part A of this problem, you studied the possibility of interpreting strings like "Bess to wear a wig," "her to be gone," and "Mary Helen's murdering her father" as simple sentences in special forms. Does this interpretation seem to coincide with the way that people comprehend sentences in which such strings occur?

3. Do you think that people might, in effect, interpret *seeing* and *believing* in "Seeing is believing" as simple sentences? If they might, what's the subject of *seeing*? Of *believing*? Does "Seeing is believing" mean something like "For someone to see something is for someone to believe something"?

4. The comprehension of language is, of course, a psychological process: speech and writing give our perception sets of signals, and our brains turn these signals into meaning. Does it follow, then, that a grammar book is, for better or worse, a hypothesis about this psychological process?

5. If the proposition in number 4 happened to be valid, how would you account for the fact that, even today, many psychologists know little about the structure of language and many linguists know little about the psychology of cognition?

6. What does this connection between language and psychology have to do with the process of learning to read?

problem 18

Deletions

A. BACKGROUND DATA

1. Whereas many preceding problems treat additions to basic sentences, this problem centers on sentences from which something seems to be missing. Let's work into it by starting with a review. In this book, I have repeatedly asked you to think about the concept of language as a system of signals of meaning. (See especially problems 4, 9, and 17.) Does it seem to you, at this point in your study of the English language, to be a valid concept? If you think not, fine. But, if you think so, the data in this problem may cause you to reconsider. We'll return to this matter later.

2. Now, let's turn to the specific feature of English sentences that may lead to this reconsideration. You often hear people tell you, "Say what you mean." Yet it is perfectly normal *not* to say everything you mean. In fact, you'd be a terrible bore if you tried it. In fact, you'd sound like you didn't know English very well. Just for an example, who'd ever think of saying this?

> We had planned to take a cruise around the Cape of Good Hope in our yacht "Sorry Lot" next November, but we can't take a cruise around the Cape of Good Hope in our yacht "Sorry Lot" next November.

Sure—that might be *what you mean*, but it's not going to be *what you say*. What *would* you say?

117

3. The English language abounds in examples like these:

a. Jarvis, aged 54, wants to marry and leave home; and his parents also want him to.
b. You're fatter than Behemoth Bob.
c. When Cletus bought five pounds of chocolates, Samantha bought some, too.
d. If you want to buy a new car, I think you should.

What do Jarvis's parents want him to do? Is Behemoth Bob fat? What did Samantha buy? What do "I" think "you" should do?

4. Now, it would be all right to say, for example, "If you want to buy a new car, I think you should buy a new car"; but we usually delete everything after *should*. Are there any requirements built into the English language about what to delete in sentences like those in exercise 3?

5. Deletions are possible in many sentences. Are there any words you can delete in the following sentences without altering any part of the meaning?

a. I am smarter than you are, but the twins are not as smart as either of us.
b. I am smart and you are, but the twins are not as smart as either of us.
c. Who is smart, and who is not smart?
d. If you know what's good for you, you *will* leave my home immediately.
e. The blue of his eyes is as blue as the blue of a clear summer sky.
f. Which way is the wind blowing?
g. She lives at the same place which Sam lives at.
h. Did you know that Fritzy is pregnant?

6. It may be interesting to reconsider in the present context a question that we first took up in problem 7. Some grammar books explain that sentences like "Run home" and "Try again" have the word *you* as "the understood subject." Is the concept of "the understood subject" a reasonable explanation of what we know about the meanings of these sentences?

7. Would it be more accurate to state that "Run home" is derived from an underlying sentence "You *will* run home" (with a command emphasis on *will*) by deleting "You will"? (An alter-

native possibility is that there is an underlying sentence "You must run home.")

8. Assuming that you accept the idea that "You will" is understood in "Run home," why is it possible to delete "You will" in "You *will* run home" but not "She will" in "She *will* run home"?

9. Some deletions have slightly different conditions from those discussed in exercises 1 to 8. For instance, what other change must you make if you delete the italicized parts of the following sentences?

    a. Isadore ran home fast, and José *ran home fast*, too.
    b. Annabel Lee thinks Poe was a second-rate poet, and the raven *thinks he was*, too.
    c. Annabel Lee thinks Poe was a second-rate poet, and the raven thinks *he was*, too.
    d. Eleanor loved Franklin, and he knew she *loved him*.

10. Here's a different situation. Does a comparison of the two sentences "Hal is worried about Virginia's winning the contest" and "Hal is worried about winning the contest" suggest that something has been deleted from the second sentence? Why can't *Virginia's* be deleted in the first?

11. At this point, let's re-examine something else you've encountered before, this time in terms of deletions. In problem 14, you were asked to consider descriptive words and phrases following nouns. You might have thought of something like "The boy singing songs likes the girl playing the zither." Do you think it makes sense to explain this sentence as deriving from three underlying simple sentences—"The boy likes the girl," "The boy is singing songs," "The girl is playing the zither"—which are first combined to produce "The boy who is singing songs likes the girl who is playing the zither" and next altered by deletion to yield "The boy singing songs likes the girl playing the zither"?

12. In exercise 2, I suggested that "the data in this problem may cause you to reconsider" the concept of language as a system of signals of meaning? Does it? Why or why not?

13. If you were stubbornly to stick to your guns, could you support the idea that, even when deletions are made, there must still be signals for the complete meanings of sentences?

14. Are deletions in English sentences strictly controlled by convention?

B. MAKING GRAMMAR

1. In this part, imagine that you are writing for someone who does not understand the conventions underlying the deletions illustrated below. With this in mind, examine these sentences.

   a. Sally wants to learn to fly, and John wants her to.
   b. Josh was told it's wrong to kill, and he believes it's so.
   c. Josh was told it's wrong to kill, and he believes it.
   d. You cheated on the exam, and I know you did.
   e. Lester said he wasn't kidding, and, sure enough, he wasn't.

2. Now, write a set of exact, concise rules which explain *where* deletions may be made and *how* they must be made.

   Collect additional data to check the validity of your rules and, if necessary, rewrite the rules.

C. GRAMMAR AND PEOPLE

1. All the deletions cited in parts A and B are standard in both spoken and written English. Can you think of any that occur in speech and written dialog but would not be likely to occur in other kinds of writing? (An example is. "See you soon.")

2. Do people ever make any deletions in friendly letters that they wouldn't make in, say, a freshman theme?

3. Many people find it difficult to read the following poem the first time. What might be the connection between their difficulty and the kinds of deletions the poet makes?

Spring and Fall:
to a Young Child

by Gerard Manley Hopkins[1]

MÁRGARÉT, áre you gríeving
Over Goldengrove unleaving?
Leáves, like the things of man, you
With your fresh thoughts care for, can you?

[1] Gerard Manley Hopkins, *The Poems* (New York: Oxford University Press, 1967), pp. 88–89.

Ah! as the heart grows older
It will come to such sights colder
By and by, nor spare a sigh
Though worlds of wanwood leafmeal lie;
And yet you *will* weep and know why.
Now no matter, child, the name:
Sorrow's springs are the same.
Nor mouth had, no nor mind, expressed
What heart heard of, ghost guessed:
It is the blight man was born for,
It is Margaret you mourn for.

4. Deletions must be rather strictly controlled in writing or else sentences will lose essential meaning. What are the conditions that make it possible for people to be so much looser and to make so many more deletions in talking? Give specific examples, please.

5. Certain dialects of English permit deletions that are not permitted in others. An example from the dialects of some black-Americans is deletion of the *be*-form before *-ing* verbs, as in "He going" as contrasted to "He is going." Does this deletion destroy any essential meaning in the sentence?

problem 19

Underlying meaning
in sentences

A. BACKGROUND DATA

1. This problem deals with other aspects of what is implicit in sentences. It's clear from the exercises you've done so far in this book that there's more to English sentences than meets the eye and ear. Some aspects are harder to see than others. Let's start with the sentence "Breathard is easy to please"—no problems. Everything is apparent, isn't it?

2. Not really. Compare these two sentences:

a. Breathard is easy to please.
b. Breathard is eager to please.

Who pleases and who gets pleased in these two sentences?

3. Is it a reasonable assumption that underlying sentence 2.a is an idea which could be stated in the form of the sentence "Someone pleases Breathard" and that underlying 2.b is "Breathard pleases someone"?

4. And notice the difference in the relationship between *MacArthur* and *return* in the first sentence below and in the second sentence:

a. MacArthur promised the people to return.
b. MacArthur convinced the people to return.

State the underlying ideas here in the form of sentences.

122

5. What features of the words *easy, eager, promised,* and *convinced* must a person know to interpret sentences 2.a, 2.b, 4.a, and 4.b?

6. Many other sentences which are similar in appearance turn out to be quite different in other respects. What difference is there in the relationship between *Jessica* and *chairman* in sentence a below and that between *Jessica* and *chair* in b?

    a. The committee named Jessica chairman.
    b. The committee gave Jessica a chair.

7. Would "The committee named Jessica to be chairman" be a reasonable substitute for sentence 6.a? Can you explain the difference in the specified relationships in exercise 6 by postulating underlying ideas in sentence-form?

8. Take another pair. Write out the underlying sentences to clarify the relationships among the words in the following:

    a. They are walking the horses.
    b. They are the walking horses.

9. Explain, in terms of underlying sentences, the difference in meaning between these two sentences:

    a. This is a finishing school.
    b. This is a finished school.

10. The idea of underlying sentences is very useful in explaining certain parts of many sentences. All the italicized items in the following sentences are compounds of two words. Explain, in terms of underlying sentences, how the two words in each compound are related:

    a. The *living-room* has *grass-green* carpet.
    b. *Status-seekers* are seldom popular.
    c. "Dr. Sunshine's Elixir" is really a *weed-killer.*
    d. *Windblown* hairstyles are popular in Chicago.
    e. *Homegrown* tomatoes are very expensive.
    f. A *man-eating* tiger lives upstairs.
    g. A *well-turned* ankle hardly turns a head nowadays.
    h. That's a *nice-looking* girdle you have on.
    i. Many people prefer *corn-fed* beef.
    j. *Chicken-fried* steak is perennial.
    k. What is a *tree-top* lover anyhow?

    l. Have you ever walked with a *street-walker?*
    m. The *firetruck* is on fire.
    n. She dyed her *fire-red* hair *ash-blond.*
    o. The *firemen* live in the *firehouse.*
    p. Does she drink *firewater* with the *fire-fighters?*
    q. *Firestone* is a *fireball.*
    r. A *fired-up* worker often makes mistakes.
    s. We live in a *tree-house* in Peoria.
    t. The *town-crier* has laryngitis.
    u. Did *cavemen* invent fire or discover it?
    v. Don't lose your *underwear.*

B. MAKING GRAMMAR

    1. Study the ambiguity of each of the following written sentences in terms of underlying sentences:

    a. Our business is growing.
    b. They are cooking apples.
    c. Which one is drinking water?
    d. Failing health has seriously upset me.
    e. Fonda enjoys entertaining men.

    The ambiguity of each of these sentences can be explained as deriving from two possible underlying sentences neither of which is clearly signalled in the actual sentence.
    2. Write a detailed account of the derivation of the actual sentences from the underlying sentences, including:

    a. A full statement of each possible underlying idea
    b. An explanation of the parts of the underlying sentences which are deleted in the actual sentences
    c. An explanation of how deletion of necessary signals produced the ambiguities
    d. A sample of how the actual sentences can be clarified by providing necessary signals of the underlying sentences.

C. GRAMMAR AND PEOPLE

    1. Would the five sentences cited in part B of this problem usually be ambiguous when spoken? Explain why or why not.

2. What aspects of meaning can the human voice provide that the printed page cannot?

3. In isolation, the sentence "They are running greyhounds" is ambiguous; it could mean either of the following:

Those people are causing greyhounds to run.
Those dogs are greyhounds which are running.

Without resorting to rewording as above or to special emphasis in speaking, can you imagine situations which will make clear the meanings intended?

4. It is very easy to invent ambiguous sentences like those in part B of this problem. How frequently do sentences that are *structurally* ambiguous (that is, you can't be sure of what the underlying sentences are) occur in everyday conversation? How frequently are they *actually* ambiguous to the listeners? Why?

5. Can you use the "mind-computer" suggested in 4.C.3 to analyze the following sentence?

They are eating the apples.

problem 20

Analysis of literal word-meaning

A. BACKGROUND DATA

1. This problem treats the meanings of the individual words which sentences are composed of, a topic which is not fully handled in the first nineteen problems of this book. These earlier problems develop the idea that a sentence is neither the words in it nor the arrangement of the words, but is rather the words in the arrangement—though this statement is not, by any means, a complete definition of *sentence*. The meanings of words and their interplay within sentences are, however, significant enough to deserve the special attention they get in this problem and the next.

2. A simple beginning: quickly jot down your own informal definitions of the words *man* and *house*.

3. Now, a slight complication: assume that a specific person says the following sentence to another specific person in a specific place—

That man lives in the pink house on the corner.

Do the definitions you wrote in exercise 2 actually define the real-life person and the real-life building to which the words *man* and *house* refer in the sentence? Explain yourself, please.

4. On the basis of what you did in exercise 3, can you distinguish two aspects to the meanings of words?

5. How are we able to make words like *man* and *house*, which

126

can denote any one of the millions of men and houses in the world, refer to the specific things we want them to refer to, as in the sample sentence in exercise 3?

6. If I use the word *man* to denote the man who is president of the United States, as in "That man couldn't find his way out of a paper bag," what is the *real* meaning of the word *man*—"an adult male human-being" or "the adult male human-being who is president of the United States"?

7. And consider the word *man* in other contexts. Does it mean the same thing in all these sentences?

a. God loves *man*.
b. Your five-year-old is quite a little *man* now.
c. *Man* must have his mate.
d. It is still popularly believed that the sexual drive of a *man* is stronger than that of a woman.
e. Hitler was a demented *man*.

8. Well, now, if *man* is not always man, were the ladies of the old-fashioned expression "*ladies* of the evening" really ladies?

9. All this thinking about *man* and *ladies* leads to one central question: what is the relationship between the meanings of words given in a dictionary and the meanings of words used in everyday conversation?

10. This question merits some careful consideration. Let's look first at the everyday usage. Many factors affect the meanings of words in daily use. Think about this. What is the meaning of *big* as it is used in these sentences?

a. That is a *big* amoeba.
b. That is a *big* ant.
c. That is a *big* caterpillar.
d. That is a *big* mouse.
e. That is a *big* rat.
f. That is a *big* dog.
g. That is a *big* horse.
h. That is a *big* elephant.
i. That is a *big* dinosaur.
j. That is a *big* mountain.
k. That is a *big* ocean.
l. That is a *big* planet.
m. That is a *big* galaxy.

How big is big anyway? (Can you answer this question any better than you could when I first asked it—in problem 2?)

11. Now, let's look at a different aspect of meaning in everyday use. Do the words *Munsingwear* and *silly* in the following sentence convey the same *kind* of information insofar as the meanings may be verified by objective data?

    a. That is a *Munsingwear* suit Jake has on.
    b. That is a *silly* suit Jake has on.

12. Which of the italicized words below convey verifiable information and which convey nonverifiable opinion?

    a. Myoshi Umeki is a *Japanese* actress.
    b. Myoshi Umeki is a *beautiful* actress.
    c. Noam Chomsky is a *genius*.
    d. Elmer Gluck is a *fool*.
    e. Lisa's new car is *green*.
    f. Lisa's new car is *sporty*.
    g. Chester Lee is a *charlatan*.
    h. Pauline is *skinny*.
    i. The cellar is made of *concrete*.
    j. It is a *humid* day.
    k. Fred has *black* hair.

13. It is often pointed out that everybody has a different meaning for the word *love*. If that's so, then how are people able to understand one another when they're talking about love?

14. We need to look in more detail at what actually constitutes the conventional meanings of words, as they are given in dictionaries. What element of meaning do the following words have in common?

    a. entity
    b. animal
    c. human-being
    d. female
    e. girl

15. In what features of meaning are the words listed in exercise 14 different?

16. List the features of meaning that each word in the following groups has in common with the other words in its group and the features in which it is different:

a	b	c
bull	house	grapefruit
man	skyscraper	tangerine
boy	gymnasium	lemon
stallion	tent	orange
gander	museum	lime

17. Can you define the features of a coyote so that a visitor to a zoo can distinguish a coyote from a dog without reading the signs on the cages?

18. Through language, the things of the world are grouped into categories—flowers, snakes, men, women, cities, houses, for example. There are often thousands of individuals in each category. What is the basic distinguishing feature of each category named by each of the following words? (With the first word—*tree*—what, for example, distinguishes the category of trees from all other categories?)

a. tree	f. grass	k. toy
b. shrub	g. weed	l. hate
c. city	h. man	m. candy
d. house	i. boy	n. cookie
e. town	j. trash	o. kindness

19. What's the difference between a *house* and a *home?* A *woman* and a *lady?* A *dog* and a *mutt?* Are the distinctions features of the meanings of the words?

20. And what about these words? What's the difference between an *economy* car and a *cheap* car? A *queer* and a *homosexual?* A *yard* and a *lawn?* An *enthusiast* and a *show-off?* A *spendthrift* and a *generous person?* An *imaginative person* and a *dreamer?* A *realist* and a *pessimist?*

B. MAKING GRAMMAR

1. As the exercises in part B indicate, the meanings of English words are a very complex matter, involving the interaction of (a) the conventional general meanings of words known or available to all speakers of English (as set down in good dictionaries—"adult male human-being," for example), (b) the specific entities and

concepts to which speakers make the words refer in specific sentences spoken in specific speech situations (for example, *man* designating Jackson Wilfred Bartholomy IV), and (c) the individual elements of meaning which the opinions of speakers add to (a) and (b) (as in "Act like a man").

2. Explain as clearly as you can the interaction of these three aspects of meaning and provide ample illustrations.

C. GRAMMAR AND PEOPLE

1. In general terms, a child must learn two basic things to master English: (a) the meanings of words and (b) the arrangements of words into sentences. On the basis of your studies in this book, which would you say is the more complex thing to learn?

2. In the introductory chapter of this book, I cited the example of a child learning the meaning of the word *garbage*. Seemingly simple at first thought, the process of learning is, in fact, rather complex. Can you think up a reasonably convincing theory of how a child develops the meaning of the word *garbage*?

3. Have you ever discovered an instance in which your idea of the meaning of a word is not that of most other people? How does this happen?

4. Think of the word that you hate most and, if you don't already know, try to figure out how you developed your hate for it.

5. Do you like your own given name(s)? Why or why not?

6. How many different ways can you say "Shut up" just by changing your tone of voice but without changing the words?

7. Someone once observed of someone else, "He can tell you to go to hell so that you'll want to catch the first train." How does someone do this?

8. What aspects of speech can convince you that someone is lying?

9. If a man in love with a pauper told you seriously, "My love is a rich, rich woman," you'd say he was lying. Was Robert Burns lying when he wrote, "O, my luve is like a red, red rose"?

problem 21

The problem of nonliteral statements

A. BACKGROUND DATA

1. In this problem, we examine another aspect of word-meaning. The word-meanings covered in 20.A are pretty literal, though we ran into some problems with what a man is and how big big is. Still, these problems are not very much like the problem of word-meaning in statements such as "O, my luve is like a red, red rose" or "That guy I dated in Houston is a dog." What's the difference?

2. The two sentences cited in exercise 1 illustrate what is traditionally called "figurative language," and many people think of figurative language as language that is used mostly in poetry. Is the use of figurative language, in fact, confined mainly to poetry?

3. What is the difference between ordinary comparisons like "The animal that chased me is like a dog" and figurative comparisons like "The boy that chased me is like a dog"? Devise your answer from these two sentences and test it on other examples.

4. Common figurative comparisons are drawn from many sources. Animals, for example, are a widely used source: "tired as a dog," "wet as a rat," "stubborn as a mule," "sly as a fox." List five examples from each of the following sources listed:

a. fruits and vegetables   d. roads and highways
b. weather   e. flowers
c. architecture and design

5. What are some other sources of figurative comparisons?

6. Just as significant as the sources of figurative comparisons are the things the comparisons are used to describe. List figurative comparisons you have heard used to describe each of the following categories:

    a. the physical appearance of people
    b. the personalities of people
    c. emotions
    d. thought-processes
    e. the actions of people

7. You could get very long lists for the categories given in exercise 6. There are hundreds of figurative comparisons for emotions and thinking, for example. Why are there so many?

8. Decide whether the italicized words in the following sentences are "literal" or "figurative" in meaning:

    a. Do you *see* what I am trying to explain?
    b. Do you *understand* what I'm saying?
    c. Inalou dropped a *head* of cabbage on her toe.
    d. When you turn onto the highway, *head* north.
    e. Balderdash is *head* of the household.
    f. Plants *breathe.*
    g. The heart *pumps* blood.
    h. Many children have been *cowed.*
    i. What is the *point* of your story?
    j. The hobo is often called *"king* of the road."
    k. The sun is *going down.*
    l. She *broke* my heart.

9. What things did you have to consider to make your decisions in exercise 8?

10. There are other kinds of statements that are not literally true. Exaggerations, for example. When someone uses an expression such as, "I took a million steps today," you know it's an exaggeration. But what if a computer operator told you, "I made a million computations today"? What is your understanding of such exaggerations dependent on—that is, how do you know an exaggeration is an exaggeration?

11. And then there's the other side. If a nineteen-year-old woman remarked of her ninety-six-year-old husband, "I married an

older man," her statement would obviously be the opposite of exaggeration (overstatement). How do you know when someone is using understatement?

12. Now, the fourth and last kind of special language we'll cover in the problem. You probably remember Antony's famous ironic line in *Julius Caesar*: "Brutus is an honorable man"; and you probably recall that he is saying the opposite of what he means. Along these same lines, I once heard someone state that a certain former president of the United States was "a good man just like Judas Iscariot was a good man." When people say such things, how do you know they mean the opposite of what their words say? What if the speaker really admired Judas?

13. How frequent in everyday conversation is the kind of ironic statement illustrated in 12?

B. MAKING GRAMMAR

1. All the kinds of meaning in problem 20 are fairly literal— the words are used in their conventional senses. Those meanings in problem 21.A involve departures of one kind or another from literal truth. Write an account of the various kinds of nonliteral uses of words examined in part A and of the means by which people manage to make their meaning clear even though they're not telling the literal truth.

C. GRAMMAR AND PEOPLE

1. The use by men of animal comparisons to describe women involves some interesting distinctions.

a. Most women would resent being referred to by the following terms in the left-hand column, but some would feel complimented by those in the right-hand column:

(1) sheep   (5) lamb
(2) cat   (6) kitten
(3) hen   (7) chick
(4) dog   (8) pup

What's the difference?

b. Would some women also resent the comparisons in the right-hand column? Why?

2. Members of the American Pork Association once waged a promotional campaign in which they sought to discredit the popular figurative comparisons involving *pig* and *hog*. Why do you suppose it didn't succeed? Do pigs deserve their reputation?

3. Do you think that psychologists could devise a valid personality test using such multiple-choice items as these?

   a. Making love is like:
      (1) taking a trip in outer space
      (2) being cornered by a vampire
      (3) being selected king or queen for a day
      (4) reading a good book
   b. My mother reminds me most of:
      (1) an orchid
      (2) a rose
      (3) a zinnia
      (4) a sunflower
   c. In the morning, I usually look ahead to the day as if it were:
      (1) a maze
      (2) another chapter in a mediocre book
      (3) a pit of vipers
      (4) a window of many-colored glass

4. To what extent are the figurative comparisons people use an index to what they are really like?

5. Is understatement or overstatement used more extensively in ordinary conversation?

6. The people of the United States are often noted for their use of pretended insults—saying things which, if taken literally, would be insulting, but saying them to friends to be amusing rather than actually insulting. Some observers claim that this use of insults is a reflection of a certain shallowness of character in that it is a way of avoiding serious, honest relationships. What do you think?

problem 22

An introduction to speech contexts

A. BACKGROUND DATA

1. Whereas problems 1 to 21 deal almost exclusively with language itself, this problem deals with some of the nonlinguistic things that accompany language in real speech situations. When you are carrying on a conversation with people, how much of the information that you get comes from what the other people say and how much from other aspects of the conversation?

2. What part does each of the following items play in a conversation?

 a. gestures c. tone of voice
 b. facial expressions

3. Are there other items that supplement language? Do the following contribute anything to the information you get in a conversation?

 a. the physical positions of people in relationship to one another
 b. the clothing of the conversants
 c. the setting
 d. the physical size and appearance of the conversants
 e. the way they sit or stand
 f. their eyes
 g. what you know of the conversants' backgrounds
 h. the rate at which they talk, their pauses, and "fillers" such as *uh* and *well*

135

4. Consider the tone of voice a bit more carefully now. Describe as specifically as you can how you might say "John is here" so as to convey each of the following states of mind:

a. anger c. disgust e. fear
b. uncertainty d. elation f. indifference

5. Next, think about some other devices that communicate. What, for instance, is the meaning of each of the following items?

a. a raised eyebrow d. an up-and-down nod of the head
b. a wink e. a whistle
c. a shrug of the shoulders

6. Many other gestures also have meanings. List as many as you can that have conventional meanings.

7. How many "obscene" gestures do you know? What makes them "obscene"?

8. Do the same gestures have the same meanings in all societies?

9. When someone says something, *exactly how* are gestures, tone of voice, and facial expressions related to the words the person says? Do gestures or facial expressions ever substitute for any of the words in sentences?

10. The elements of language itself—sounds, words, sentences—operate systematically. Are gestures, tone of voice, and facial expressions also systematic?

B. MAKING GRAMMAR

1. Write an account of how the following items *interact* in a conversation:

a. language
b. tone of voice
c. gestures
d. facial expressions
e. physical positions
f. setting

2. Please provide examples to clarify your comments.

C. GRAMMAR AND PEOPLE

1. Often, two-thirds or more of what we get out of a face-to-face conversation comes from the nonverbal sources identified in part A of this problem, leaving one-third to language itself. Listen to and watch someone saying something—note the language and the nonverbal aspects. Then replay the scene in your mind, imagining it without the language. How does the *communication* hold up in your replay?

2. Replay the speech you observed in doing exercise 1, this time as a telephone speech. What changes would the speaker have to make to adapt to a situation in which the effectiveness of the communication must be achieved strictly by sound?

3. Ask some people who were born in the early 1930s and who listened to radio before 1949 to name some of the radio stars that tried but did not make it in television. Did the failure of any of them in television have anything to do with the aspects of communication treated in this problem?

4. Is the eye-contact which is vital to our conversation similarly valued in all other societies?

5. In our society, it is generally considered "sissy" for one man to slap another on the face. Has it always been so regarded?

6. How far away do you prefer another person to stay from you when talking to you? Why? Can a person stay too far away, though within hearing-range, for you to converse?

7. Does it bother you for another person to converse with you while he or she is doing some written work such as filling out a form or recopying notes? Why?

8. Have you ever read anything about the "psychology" of the design of Gothic cathedrals? If not, check into it and consider what you read in terms of the topic of this problem.

9. To what extent and in what ways are people's homes expressions of the people themselves?

10. By what signs do you know that someone likes or dislikes you? Are any of the elements discussed in this problem relevant in such decisions?

problem 23

The basis of traditional grammar

A. BACKGROUND DATA

1. In the twenty-two preceding problems in this book, you have been doing exactly the kind of things that professional grammarians do: studying examples of the language that people use and devising explanations of how sentences are put together to communicate meaning.

Of course, you aren't so highly trained as most grammarians, and your explanations haven't been so detailed as theirs; nevertheless, your work and theirs have been toward the same end.

One difference may not have been obvious to you. Whereas many of your explanations have been "commonsense" explanations, professional grammarians—linguists, as they're known today—try to formulate their explanations in terms of one *theory of language* or another.

A theory of language is generally just like any other theory. There have been through the years, for example, many theories about human behavior. The behavior itself is a fact—we see it and we do it. But the how and why of it are not so apparent, and psychologists make up theories about them and test and retest their theories against actual behavior. In the Renaissance, the main theory was that human beings were physically composed of four fluids and that behavioral differences were due to the proportions of these fluids in relationship to one another—if a person had a pre-

138

dominance of a particular one, he would be melancholy, whereas a predominance of another fluid produced a fiery tempered person. Though this seems rather crude to us, it is nevertheless a theory. Additional biochemical knowledge about human beings, of course, proved it wrong. Today, a very popular theory of human behavior is that differences are due to a combination of inherited traits and conditioning by environment.

Along the same lines, the *structure* of language, like human behavior, is itself a fact—it is a real part of language, built in; and we master and use it without thinking much about it. On the other hand, a *grammar*, as I defined the term on page one ("an explanation of the way language is put together") and as I have used it throughout this book in the phrase "making grammar," is really a *theory* about how language operates.

And, in the study of language, as in the study of human behavior, various theories have come and gone. The theory which predominated in grammatical study for a long time is commonly called "traditional grammar." Examination of some of the key concepts of traditional grammar is the topic of this problem. The concepts introduced are ones that were used for years in a majority of school textbooks. Many other traditional concepts, excellent by modern standards, did not turn up in textbooks. You are most likely, of course, to be familiar with the textbook ideas; and, for this reason, I deal with them only.

2. The central concept of traditional school grammar is stated in this definition: "A sentence is a group of words having a subject and a predicate and expressing a complete idea." The terms *subject* and *predicate* will be treated in one of the following exercises; here, let's examine the idea of a complete idea—how would you define a *complete idea?*

   a. Examine the following groups of words:
      (1) It is his.
      (2) Esau running around tearing his hair and screaming about his birthright.

Are both (1) and (2) sentences? Does either express by itself "a complete idea"? If neither, which comes closer?

   b. Does any of the following sentences express a complete idea?
      (1) They cannot find it in there.
      (2) If that is true, then the other cannot be.

(3) John F. Kennedy was not much of a philosopher.
(4) Lisa Lou is one, too.
(5) The whole is equal to the sum of its parts.

3. The words which compose the "group" referred to in the definition of a sentence cited in exercise 2—"A sentence is a group of words having a subject and a predicate and expressing a complete idea"—are usually classified, in a traditional grammar, into eight parts of speech: noun, pronoun, verb, adjective, adverb, preposition, conjunction, and interjection. You analyzed definitions of these terms in problem 3; it might be helpful to review your work there.

4. The traditional definition designates that the sentence consists of a subject and a predicate. The subject is usually defined as "that part of the sentence about which something is stated" and the predicate as "that part of the sentence which does the stating." How precise are these definitions?

a. In the sentence "I have completely ruined my brand-new Pogo stick," *I* is the subject. Does it make sense to claim that the sentence states more about *I* than about "my brand-new Pogo stick," which is part of the predicate? Is the actual intent of this sentence something like "My brand-new Pogo stick is the thing which I have completely ruined"?

b. And how would you treat such common sentences as "It is raining" and "It is snowing"? Of course, *it* is not the subject in these sentences as *it* is in "It is mine." But what is the subject if *it* isn't?

c. Come on—try one more: "The woman picking her teeth is my friend." The subject is generally considered to be "The woman picking her teeth" and the predicate to be "is my friend." Still, doesn't "picking her teeth" state something about "the woman"? What's the problem? Are "the woman" and "picking her teeth" a subject and a predicate *within* the subject "the woman picking her teeth"?

5. Another sentence element, in traditional grammar a part of the predicate, is the *direct object,* which is defined as "the receiver of the action of the verb." In connection with a sentence such as "Myrtle slapped Snerdmore," Snerdmore will verify the definition. But is it accurate to state that *picture* is literally a receiver of action in the sentence "Mossbottom saw the picture"?

And what about *gas* in "I smell gas"? And *noise* in "I hear a strange noise"? And *lessons* in "I know my lessons"?

6. In traditional grammar, the string "That skinny woman is married to a man" as part of the sentence "That skinny woman is married to a man who is very fat" is called the *independent clause,* and "who is very fat" is called the *dependent clause.* Are the terms *independent clause* and *dependent clause* accurate?

7. The distinction between independent and dependent clauses presents problems. Compare these two sentences:

    a. Frederick plays well though he is crippled.
    b. Frederick plays well but he is crippled.

Is there any significant difference in meaning between them?

8. In traditional grammar, "though he is crippled" in 7.a is called a dependent clause; and "but he is crippled" in 7.b is called an independent clause. Is this distinction logically defensible?

9. In connection with the clauses "though he is crippled" and "but he is crippled" in exercise 7, what happens if you try to move them into position before "Frederick plays well"? Is the only significant difference between them a matter of mobility?

10. And look at another idea about clauses. Do these two sentences mean basically the same thing?

    a. That John is chasing cars is common knowledge.
    b. John's chasing cars is common knowledge.

11. In traditional grammar, "That John is chasing cars" is called a clause; but "John's chasing cars" is a phrase. Is this a valid distinction?

12. A traditional analysis of the string "John's chasing cars" in sentence 10.b would read something like this: *"John's* is a possessive noun modifying *chasing; chasing* is an *-ing* verb form functioning as a noun (a gerund) and used as the subject of *is; cars* is the object of the gerund *chasing."* Does this analysis omit any information necessary to understanding the real relationship among the words *John's, chasing,* and *cars?* Would it make more sense to analyze the three parts as something like a subject (*John's*), a verb (*chasing*), and a direct object (*cars*)?

13. There are other similar problems. In the sentence "Jezebel thinks that smoking is fun," a traditional analysis would note

only that *smoking* is a gerund used as the subject of *is*. Does it seem a defect in the analysis that it does not indicate in any way what everyone who understands the sentence knows—the underlying idea that it is Jezebel's smoking that is fun to Jezebel?

14. Application of the traditional theory of the sentence yields something like the following analysis of the sentence "The girl singing is my best friend":

    a. The sentence consists of one independent clause.

    b. In the independent clause "The girl singing is my best friend":
        (1) *the* is an article modifying *girl*,
        (2) *girl* is a singular common noun, functioning as the subject of *is*,
        (3) *singing* is a present participle modifying *girl*,
        (4) *is* is a linking verb, present tense, third-person singular,
        (5) *my* is a possessive adjective modifying *friend*,
        (6) *best* is an adjective, superlative degree, modifying *friend*,
        (7) *friend* is a singular common noun, functioning as the predicate nominative, renaming *girl* to provide additional identification.

Consider just one specific question: is the statement that "*singing* is a present participle modifying *girl*" an adequate explanation of the understood relationship between *girl* and *singing*?

15. I have deliberately aimed your work in this problem at some of the more questionable aspects in the theory of traditional grammar because I believe that thinking about what the theory covers and what it does not cover that it ought to is an effective way of understanding what the function of a grammar is—explanation of how language works. However, it is also effective to think about what changes might be made in traditional theory to enable it to cover some of the things it ought to but does not cover—and that is the topic of problem 24.

B. MAKING GRAMMAR

1. In this assignment, you are asked to be both critical and creative. The traditional definition of the sentence—"a group of words having a subject and a predicate and expressing a complete idea"—is, as your work in part A demonstrates, weak. Using this awareness, do the following:

a. Write a detailed criticism of the traditional definition, pointing out both strengths and weaknesses.

b. If you can, write a better definition and demonstrate how it is better. If you cannot write a demonstrably better definition, explain why you cannot.

C. GRAMMAR AND PEOPLE

1. A grammar should explain something about how people comprehend language. Does the portion of traditional grammar presented in this problem meet this requirement?

2. It is implied in exercise 12 of part A of this problem that the traditional analysis of *John's* in "John's chasing cars is common knowledge" as "a possessive noun modifying *chasing*" is inadequate in that it does not state explicitly that the structure "John's chasing cars" is equivalent in meaning to "John is chasing cars." Must people understand the idea that John is chasing cars to understand the whole sentence?

3. Some theories close doors to thinking, and others open doors and lead to further thinking. Traditional grammar is a theory about language. But what kind of theory is it? Would you say that *accepting* the traditional analyses examined in this problem has the effect on people who are studying the English language of stymying thought—that is, that taking the analyses at face-value will cause students to fail to discover some significant underlying processes in human comprehension of language? Or will it open doors?

4. Do you think that there will ever be a grammar that accounts for all the things that we must know to understand the English language? Why?

5. What is the greatest problem both in understanding the mental processes by which people comprehend language and also in understanding human psychological processes in general?

6. Do you think that, despite the problems involved, it is worthwhile to make grammatical theories and general psychological theories? Why?

7. What cautions would you issue to people who make such theories? To those who read such theories?

problem 24

Revising traditional grammar

A. BACKGROUND DATA

1. Despite the negative emphasis in problem 23, some modern linguists have found many workable ideas in traditional grammar. In fact, most of the traditional analyses examined in that problem can be *greatly* improved with just a *little* doctoring. "Doctoring" is the goal of this problem.

Let's start with the traditional definition of a sentence—"a group of words having a subject and a predicate and expressing a complete idea." Clearly, the claim that a sentence expresses a complete idea is nonsense, as the examples in 23.A.2 show. Would it come nearer the truth to insert the word *grammatically* before *complete*: "a grammatically complete idea"?

2. "Grammatical completeness" is no easy concept to define in itself. However, it strikes me as one that's easier to get hold of than "a complete idea." For example, if I plan to say a sentence that concerns the action of "giving," the system of the English language requires me to do certain things to achieve "grammatical completeness":

> a. In the action of giving, three noun-ideas are always involved: the giver, that which is given, and the receiver. I must always either name or clearly imply the second noun-idea—"that which is given"—and almost always name one of the other two and ordinarily the third also:

144

(1)   Giver   Receiver Given
     | | |

   Margaret gave *Celeste a ring.*

(2) *Margaret* gave *a ring.*

(3) *Celeste* was given *a ring* by *Margaret.*

(4) *Celeste* was given *a ring.*

(5) *A ring* was given *Celeste.*

(6) *A ring* was given.

  b. I must select one noun-idea as the subject.

  c. I must make the verb phrase have certain forms (*give / gives, gave, will / shall give, has given, is giving,* among others) rather than other forms (*giving, given, to give,* and so forth); and I must make the first word in the verb phrase agree in number with the subject:

    (1) She gives / is giving / has given, . . .

    (2) They give / are giving / have given, . . .

    Take it from there:

  d. If I use any nouns like *boy, horse, sugar,* and *feed* in a sentence like "_____ is here" what kind of word must precede each?

  e. If I want to use an adjective to apply a certain descriptive feature to one of the nouns such as *boy* or *feed,* where am I required to put it?

  f. Is an adjective required to make the sentence about "giving" grammatically complete?

3. Take specific directions and make a sentence about giving:

  a. Use *girl* as "giver," *catnip* as "given," and *cat* as "receiver."

  b. Indicate by choice of a word before each that all three are specifically known to the listener.

  c. Make "giver" the subject.

  d. Make the verb phrase indicate that the action is in progress at the time the sentence is said.

  e. Put "receiver" in first-object position and "given" in second-object position.

What's the result?

4. Another problematic aspect of the traditional definition is the concept of the subject—as 23.A.4 illustrates, the idea that it is "that part of the sentence about which something is stated" won't always hold water.

From the structural point of view, however, the concept of subject is no great problem. If *girl* is to be the subject and *sing* the verb, what will be the form of the verb when *girl* is singular in number? Plural in number?

Examine the following sentences and define *subject* as far as its grammatical relationship to the verb is concerned:

a. The girl sings.	k. The girl sang.
b. The girls sing.	l. The girls sang.
c. The girl is singing.	m. The girl will sing.
d. The girls are singing.	n. The girls will sing.
e. The girl was singing.	o. The girl had sung.
f. The girls were singing.	p. The girls had sung.
g. The girl has sung.	q. The girl had been singing.
h. The girls have sung.	r. The girls had been singing.
i. The girl has been singing.	s. I am singing.
j. The girls have been singing.	t. He is singing.

5. Then there's the problem of clauses. Should the terms *independent* and *dependent* in reference to clauses be amended to *structurally independent* and *structurally dependent*? If so, how would you define the amended terms?

6. If, in 23.A.14, you decided that it is not adequate to explain *singing* in the sentence "The girl singing is my best friend" as "a present participle modifying *girl*," what would you add to make the explanation adequately cover the understood relationship between *girl* and *singing*?

B. MAKING GRAMMAR

1. Exercises 10 to 13 in problem 23 deal with the traditional analysis of gerunds—*ing* verb-forms used as nouns:

a. *John's chasing cars* (in "John's chasing cars is common knowledge.")

b. *Smoking* (in "Jezebel thinks that smoking is fun.")

You will recall that, traditionally, *chasing* in sentence a is said to be a gerund used as the subject of *is* and *John's* is said to be a possessive noun modifying *chasing;* and *smoking* in sentence b is said to be a gerund used as the subject of *is.*

Retain these analyses, and, by making additions to them, write what you consider to be a more nearly adequate explanation of the implicit relationships among *John's, chasing,* and *cars* in sentence a and between *Jezebel* and *smoking* in sentence b. You may want to incorporate the idea of underlying sentences from problems 18 and 19.

C. GRAMMAR AND PEOPLE

1. Is the concept of "underlying" (or "understood" or "implicit") relationships in sentences getting to be a little too much for you? Is it justifiable to assume that so much is implied but not stated in sentences?

2. When you see the string "Bertram is a rat" written down, you can determine that, structurally, it is a complete sentence. What if someone were saying it, however, and his voice did not rise and fall at the end to indicate a completed statement and did not rise and stop to indicate a question, but instead rose, fell slightly, and hung momentarily in mid-air—would "Bertram is a rat" be a complete sentence then?

3. Imagine the following conversation:

TOM: I went downtown this morning.
RALPH: You did?
TOM: You see Paul?
RALPH: Yeah.
TOM: Was he ugly as ever?
RALPH: He was.

Are the following lines sentences? "You did?" "You see Paul?" "He was." And what about "Yeah"?

4. People have been doctoring traditional grammar for almost two hundred years. Do you think it's time we abandoned it and looked for a new theory to explain linguistic comprehension?

problem 25

The premises of two modern grammars

A. BACKGROUND DATA

In problems 23 and 24, you worked with "traditional grammar," the theory which predominated in grammatical study for almost two centuries. Doctored and doctored again, it was the main theory grammarians used in their studies and the main theory teachers taught in schools. In part C of problem 24, I asked you whether you thought it was time to stop doctoring it, abandon it, and look for a new theory to explain linguistic comprehension. Many linguists answered "yes" a long time ago; and, in the last forty years, "new" theories have developed rapidly. This problem deals with the two theories that have received the most attention since the early 1950s: structural grammar (also called *structural linguistics*) and generative-transformational grammar (popularly known as *transformational grammar*).

This problem has a somewhat different purpose from that of problems 1 to 24. Whereas the preceding problems are designed to get you to think about the main features of English structure and to make your own grammar, this problem is designed to get you to examine the chief assumptions of these two theories. Consequently, the format is slightly different.

The background data is two general articles, one setting forth the basic concepts of structural grammar, the other sketching the

148

framework of transformational grammar. Each is accompanied by questions relating to the basic premises involved.

There is no section on "making grammar," as in the other problems; because the goal is evaluation, part B is "Evaluating Grammar" and is an evaluative writing assignment.

The Structural Revolution[1]

Miriam Goldstein Sargon

1) Both revolution and counterrevolution have had a healthy effect on language study. There is a good deal of questioning, bewilderment, and debate; a good deal of unlearning and learning going on these days. No one text or school of grammar provides all the answers; but the general direction has been away from the arbitrariness and prescriptiveness of schoolroom grammars to the reasonableness and descriptiveness of scholarly traditional grammar, structural grammar, and transformational grammar; from sentence analysis to sentence building, from rote memorizing to problem solving. As a science, grammar's unsolved problems and new frontiers challenge teacher, student, and theoretician.

2) The grammar underlying the wonderful feat of language is yet to be presented in its entirety. Meanwhile there are several grammars. *A* grammar is to *the* grammar as a map is to the landscape. The road map serves one purpose, the contour map another. So is it with the various kinds of grammar now being offered. Each attempts to describe the rules underlying an English sentence; each can be evaluated in various ways; for example, by seeing how well it corresponds to the given data. Traditional classroom grammars, in their prescriptions, described how English conformed to the logic and perfection of Latin and how we might perpetuate that perfection. If, for example, you could not split an infinitive

[1] Miriam Goldstein Sargon, "The Structural Revolution," in *The Teaching of Language in Our Schools* (New York: Macmillan Publishing Company, 1966), pp. 80–90. Copyright © 1966 by the National Council of Teachers of English. Reprinted by permission of the publisher and the author.

like *amāre* into two words in the Latin language, then you should not hasten the deterioration of English which (alas!) has a two-word infinitive (to love). You should try not to further split the poor English infinitive. Scholarly traditional grammar, a natural outgrowth of traditional descriptive linguistics, is our richest source of detailed and varied examples of English sentence structure. It neatly organizes these examples, comments on them, and suggests how the student may construct similar sentences. All modern grammarians are still mining Otto Jespersen's seven-volume English grammar, one of the richest storehouses of examples of English sentences, one of the most provocative sources of modern theorizing. Jespersen's summary chapter in his *Essentials of English Grammar*,[2] for example, anticipates Charles C. Fries' analysis of grammatical devices. His chapters on junction and nexus have been picked up and expanded by transformationalists. The first stage of the revolution, then, is reflected in these early twentieth-century scholarly grammarians like Jespersen, Curme, Poutsma, and Palmer. Although some of these grammars originally taught English to foreigners, they still enlarge the understanding and appreciation of a language already known to many readers. Porter Perrin's texts (e.g., *Writer's Guide and Index to English*) incorporate much of this traditional grammar.[3] In many schools grammar is being quietly well taught through them. In others teachers are adapting to their students' level the rich fund of knowledge in Ralph B. Long's *The Sentence and Its Parts,* which incorporates contemporary scholarship in a traditional grammar.[4] What characterizes the best teaching of traditional grammar is the reformulation of knowledge. Scholarly traditional grammars always base their appreciation and prescription of an exhaustive description of spoken as well as written English.

3)   The second stage of the development of linguistics—an outcome of the awareness of linguistic relativity, of differences in languages—sought to explain the uniqueness of each system. Structural linguists collected, classified, ob-

---

[2] Otto Jespersen, *Essentials of English Grammar* (University, Alabama: University of Alabama Press, 1964).

[3] Porter G. Perrin, *Writer's Guide and Index to English,* 4th ed. (Chicago: Scott, Foresman and Company, 1965).

[4] Ralph B. Long, *The Sentence and Its Parts* (Chicago: University of Chicago Press, 1961).

served stretches of physical events called utterances as the botanist collects, observes, classifies plant life. The most subjective element in language making is obviously meaning; hence the structuralist not only refused to rely on meaning but he tried to exclude meaning from his analysis. The words "You drive me wild" may be a plea to a coy mistress or a blast at a termagant wife. The shift in meaning may interest all the neighbors, each of whom may have his theory as to how the transformation occurred. The grammarian also wants to find out how the change took place. In investigating the change, he cannot ignore the fact that speech is primary and has more signals of meaning than the written word has. Thus, though the written words remain the same, the spoken words have reversed their original meaning. But meaning is the outcome, not the method, of the structuralists.

4)   Closely related to the problem of meaning is that of criteria for classifying elements of the sentence. Here the classroom grammars proved only circular, contradictory, and confusing. A sentence, we were told, is a group of words expressing a complete thought. But who tells the child what a complete thought is? How does he know? And if he already knows, of what further use is the definition? Or a sentence is a group of words beginning with a capital letter and ending with a period. The child can accept or recognize this in his reading. But how is he to use this definition to help him in his writing? Yet we speak and are understood without punctuation. The pupil who writes sentence fragments and run-on sentences has no trouble communicating orally. He knows more about a sentence than its traditional definition.

5)   We can readily see *why* grammarians relied so heavily on meaning for classifying words as parts of speech. Since so many of our words had lost their characteristic inflections (case endings for nouns, personal and tense endings for verbs), we could no longer define them by form and meaning, as the Latinate grammars had. So we were left with meaning. *A noun is the name of a person, place or thing.* Again, because the native speaker unconsciously knows more than this definition tells him, he rarely gets into trouble. Is a thing an action like *explosion,* an event like *revolution,* a quality like *mercy,* an animal like *dinosaur,* an object like

protoplasm? Then why are *set* and *function* nouns? Note
that my question does not include the possibility that *set*
and *function* are nouns. It simply makes me seek a better
definition of noun than the semantic one. And if a verb shows
action or a state of being, where shall we draw the line
between showing an action and naming it? In *They saw the*
fireworks, where is the action? The interjection, according
to prescriptive grammars, shows strong feeling. In *She*
adores him, adores certainly expresses her strong feeling.
Is it therefore an interjection?

6)   If meaning was an unreliable criterion for some parts of
speech, might overlapping the categories of function and
meaning clarify our definitions? An adjective is a word that
modifies a noun or a pronoun. But when *A bee stung Johnny*
and me, both of us were modified by that bee. Is *bee* therefore an adjective? What does *modify* mean? An adverb is a
word that modifies a verb, adjective, or another adverb.
In *What did your brother's keeper use last year instead of*
his own money? brother becomes an adjective, *your* an adverb, *year* an adverb, *last* an adverb. A pronoun takes the
place of a noun. In *She and I are friends,* what noun does *I*
replace? In *Nelson is my hideaway; I do my writing there,* is
there a pronoun? If a conjunction is a word that connects
words, phrases, or clauses, what shall I label conjunction in
He went from pillar to post? And if a preposition is a word
that shows the relationship between its object and some
other word in the sentence, then in *John loves Mary, loves*
must be a preposition. Since all of these definitions combine
function and meaning, we do not know which takes prece-
dence—according to the definition. Yet you know and I
know in spite of the definition.

7)   Because of these problems, structuralists decided that
form and position were more reliable guides to function and
meaning. Word order was paramount: *Man bites dog* makes
headlines; *Dog bites man* is hardly news. But word order
in turn demanded classification or identification of words.
Structuralists recognized four large unlimited form classes
(noun [and pronoun], verb, adjective, and adverb) and called
the rest structure or function words (including determiners,
such as *a, an, the,* auxiliaries, intensifiers, prepositions,
conjunctions). We memorize function words naturally because they are limited in number and rarely change, yet

through their position in the sentence they show structural relationships among the form classes that signal meaning. The ambiguity of headlines or telegrams disappears when we insert a function word like *the: Jam sticks in his throat* or *Police walk nightly.* So form and word order give a sentence its structure or grammatical meaning, which in turn is the basis for its lexical meaning.

8)   In a sequence like *A raglump propagoodle hieraddles the aleurest ptolomaniacs ptaly,* the only two words that are unmistakably English are *a* and *the,* the only recognizable suffixes *-est* and *-ly.* Though there is an antique flavor about the roots of some of the other words, and *gl, mp,* and *dle* suggest the tone, we don't know what the sentence means. Yet the structural meaning is not so elusive. We can assume that what follows *a* and *the* are either nouns or noun phrases. Furthermore, the first noun phrase has to stop before *hieraddles,* because *a* signals a singular noun. So although *hieraddles* might have been a plural noun ending in *es,* and preceded by two adjectives (or what else?), it is more probably a singular verb ending in *-es* with the preceding three-word noun phrase as subject. What follows *hieraddles* now looks like another noun phrase used as an object. *Aleurest* looks like an adjective in the superlative degree just as *ptaly* looks like an adverb; its position before the noun phrase used as object confirms our suspicion. We can assume all these things if the stress and pitch and pauses go along with this analysis. We can assume that the sentence consists of subject and predicate; that the subject consists of a noun phrase, the predicate consists of a verb, noun phrase used as object, and finally adverb, as in the sentence *A rabid demagogue addles the weakest voters usually.* Given punctuation, we might also see in these words a noun series consisting of *A raglump propagoodle,* (some) *hieraddles, THE aleurest,* (some) *ptolomaniacs,* and (a little bit of) *ptaly,* as in *a Santa Claus, gifts, the tree, cones, holly.*

9)   To parse this sentence or noun phrase we have availed ourselves of the structuralists' criteria: inflectional endings, derivational prefixes and suffixes, word order, associated function words, and the suprasegmentals known as stress, pitch, and juncture or pause. In other words, by substituting the form classes and structure words in a test frame, we

have arrived either at the sentence pattern or at the noun phrase pattern. These problems were clearly faced in such revolutionary texts as Smith and Trager's *Outline of English Structure* in 1951[5] and in Fries' *The Structure of English* a year later.

10)   Inflectional endings alone are no guide, but combined with other criteria, they confirm our intuitions about the way an English sentence goes. Nouns, for example, remain unchanged except for the possessive *-'s* or *-s'* and they usually form their plurals by adding *-s* or *-es* to the singular. In some words, replacement of an internal vowel by another (man, men) functions as a grammatical signal for the plural. Verbs are usually identified by their *-ed, -t,* and *-d* endings for the past tense (or by the vowel replacement as in sang and s*i*ng) and by *-s* or *-es* for the third person singular in the present. When adjectives form their comparative and superlative by inflectional endings, those endings are *-er* and *-est*. Adverbs add the inflectional ending *-ly* to the adjective and *-er* or *-est* for comparative and superlative.

11)   In addition to inflectional endings for case, number, person, tense, and degree, the four form classes have characteristic derivational endings: prefixes or suffixes. The most common noun endings are *-hood, -acy, -tion, -age, -al, -ant, -ism, -ness, -ess, -ist, -ster, -dom, -ment, -ence, -or,* and *-er* as in *motherhood, democracy, attention, portage, survival, informant, totalitarianism, kindness, actress, jurist, youngster, kingdom, judgment, competence, actor,* and *teacher*. Verb prefixes may be *un-, be-, de-, re-, pre-,* or *dis-* as in *UNdo, BEdevil, DEcontaminate, REsell, PREview,* or *DISapprove;* suffixes may be *-ize, -ate, -fy, -en* as in *agonIZE, activATE, rareFY, threatEN*. Adjectives have a long list of derivational suffixes, identifiable in words like *ghostLY, attractIVE, goldEN, cloudY, cloudED, hesitANT, competENT, beautiFUL, courageOUS, personAL, stationARY, argumentaTIVE, childISH, fashionABLE;* the commonest prefixes are *un-, a-, in-* as in *UNkind, Amoral, INeffectual*. The commonest derivational endings for adverbs are the suffixes *-ward, -time, -wise,* and *-ly* as in *homeWARD, someTIME, otherWISE,* and *heavenLY*. All of these derivational endings show us how a part of speech is derived from the root of the

[5] Henry Lee Smith, Jr. and George L. Trager, *Outline of English Structure* (New York: American Council of Learned Societies, 1951).

word: *agonY, agonIZE, agonizING, agonizingLY,* or *rariTY, rareFY, rare, rareLY.* In *rare* the adjective shows no derivational ending. These formal contrasts signal different meanings in *the dog's friendLY arrivAL* and *the dog's friend arrivED.*

12)   But beyond inflectional and derivational ending, the four form classes can be identified by their position in the sentence and by associated function words. The usual patterns for nouns are shown in *The BABY woke, The BABY woke his MOTHER, The BABY woke his MOTHER at NIGHT, His MOTHER called the BABY a BRAT, and His MOTHER gave the BABY a BOTTLE. DICKY cried and MOTHERHOOD bored her* suggest some modifications to our tests for noun, since they do not ordinarily form plurals or take determiners like *a* or *the.* A *criminal lawyer* loses its ambiguity when we hear the stress.

13)   The most common verb patterns are *The baby DRANK his milk, The baby CRIED loudly, The baby IS hungry.* If nouns are usually signaled by determiners, verbs are often preceded by auxiliaries like *be, have, do, can, will, may, shall, must,* and *ought.* Another way to distinguish noun from verb is stress. Listen to the difference between *con'duct* and *conduct', im'port* and *import'.* Noun compounds seem to follow the pattern of initial stress, as in *mad'house, egg'head, gun'powder, air'port, mas'termind.* Verb auxiliaries have week stress except for *may, ought,* and *do.* Pause makes further syntactic distinctions. For example, it tells whether Herman is being spoken to or about in *Herman, the hermit is gone* and *Herman the hermit is gone.*

14)   Similarly adjectives and adverbs are identified by position, associated words, and stress. Adjectives usually occupy positions as in *The dog is FIERCE. The FIERCE dog snarled. They thought him DANGEROUS.* Adjectives are often preceded by intensifiers; the same is true of adverbs. Stress frequently marks the difference between adverb and preposition: *He went up. He went up the stairs.* Or adverb and conjunction: *Speak to him; however, you'll offend him. However you speak to him, you'll offend him.*

15)   Thus youngsters nowadays discover the word order or patterns which characterize the most common English sentences and which form the basis for more complicated sentences. Drill in such patterns is particularly helpful to

those who are learning English as a second language. In these patterns, parts of speech appearing in parentheses may or may not appear in the sentence. Contrast, for example, *Experience* in pattern 1 with *(The) Experience* in patterns 6 and 7.

1. (Det Noun   + Intransitive Verb + (Adv.)
   Experience   *teaches*   *occasionally*
2. (Det) Noun   + Verb   + (Det) Noun
   Experience   *teaches*   *a lesson*
3. (Det) Noun   + Linking Verb + (Det) Noun
   Experience   *is*   *a teacher*
4. (Det) Noun   + Linking Verb + Adjective
   Experience   *is*   *costly*
5. (Det) Noun   + Verb   + (Det) Noun   + (Det) Noun
   Experience   *taught*   *the boys*   *a lesson*
6. (Det) Noun   + Verb   + (Det) Noun   + (Det) Noun
   (The) Experience *made*   *the boys*   *men*
7. (Det) Noun   + Verb   + (Det) Noun   + Adjective
   (The) Experience *made*   *the boys*   *cautious*

16)   The child learns to identify clusters of nouns consisting of a headword and various modifiers—such as determiners, adjectives, participles, adverbs, prepositional phrases, and clauses—each of which occupies a fairly predictable position in the sentence. Thus we say *A certain pretty little green-eyed girl with tawny skin that suggested her creole background,* and we know that the same details in another order alter the meaning: *A pretty certain green-eyed little tawny creole girl with skin that suggested her background.* The structuralists get at the complexity of analyzing and writing mature sentences by isolating layers of structural relationships from the largest cluster (or groups of words) to the smallest morpheme (units of meaning within the word), always correlating form with order.

17)   Two great virtues of this grammar are the stress on inductive rather than deductive reasoning and the emphasis on synthesis rather than analysis. The pupil decides why he is calling a certain word a noun; he can account for his choice; he does not resort to rote memorizing or to unintelligent guessing. He also builds sentences from slots and patterns rather than takes given sentences apart. These sentences can grow in complexity as his need for expression develops. Sometimes, to wean him from earlier notions about parts of speech, he uses numbers rather than letters: *1*—noun, *2*—verb, *3*—adjective, *4*—adverb, *A*—auxiliary, *D*—determiner, *P*—preposition.

18)   To make for sharper distinctions, nouns are indexed *a, b, c,* and so forth. The first noun in a sentence is indexed *"a."* All other nouns which refer back to this noun are also indexed *"a."* (*Mother is a teacher: 1a 2 D 1a;* but *Mother saw the teacher: 1a 2 D 1b.*) When he has almost completed a standard text like Paul Roberts' *Patterns of English* (written for college freshmen but now used in junior high grades),[6] he can write sentences from formulas, for example:

A   D   1ª   2   D   1ᵇ   D   1ᶜ
Does the doctor give every patient these pills?
or
let's   2   P   D   1ª   S   D   1ᵇ   ↔   2   4
Let's get to the theater before the feature starts tonight.

where *S* = subordinator and ↔ ties units into agreement. We need only compare the definitions of *adjective, modify,* and *exclamatory sentence* in a book like James Sledd's *A Short Introduction to English Grammar*[7] with those in another text for teachers, Robert Pooley's *Teaching English Grammar,*[8] to see the structuralists' enormous advances in consistency and precision.

19)   The pupil notices the effect of various kinds of sentences —statements, questions, and requests—on the hearer. He traces these responses back to their cause in the different structure words that have signaled the sentence pattern.

20)   These criteria of word order, inflectional and derivational endings, associated function words, suprasegmentals, and sentence patterns account for the different meanings of the same word. As native speakers, we know intuitively that *about* has several different meanings in the following sentences. We don't even need to refer to a dictionary:

1. He is *about* to jump.
2. She is *about* ten years old.
3. We talked *about* ten cave men.

[6] Paul Roberts, *Patterns of English* (New York: Harcourt, Brace and World, 1956).

[7] James Sledd, *A Short Introduction to English Grammar* (Chicago: Scott, Foresman and Company, 1959).

[8] Robert C. Pooley, *Teaching English Grammar* (New York: Appleton-Century-Crofts, 1957).

4. We were given instructions *about* the work.
5. We wandered *about* the cave.
6. The railing *about* the tower is rusty.
7. I'm *about* ready to leave.
8. We moved the furniture *about* the room.
9. I spun *about*.

But in order to explain this intuitive knowledge, we need only examine the forms of words and their positions in these different contexts. Then we see how grammatical structure eliminates ambiguity. For example, *about* means *ready* only when it is followed by an infinitive. *About* means *approximately* when it is preceded by *is* and followed by countable nouns. When preceded by a verb of mental action like *talks* and followed by countable nouns, *about* means *concerning*. When preceded by a verb of physical action like *moved*, *about* means *around*. Grammatical structure, in other words, is an important part of what we loosely call *context*. . . .

21)   Structural grammar had not answered all the questions it set out to answer as to how we recognize and produce sentences, nor had it avoided all the pitfalls of semantically based grammar; but it liberated pupil and teachers from dull repetition and arbitrary routine. Structural grammar replaced the fictitious simplicity of a dead language with the complex reality of a living language. Careful observation, classification, and verification were beginning to make order out of chaos.

Questions about "The Structural Revolution"

Below are questions to direct your attention to the main concepts of structural grammar as presented in Sargon's article.

a. Sargon charges the traditional grammar such as problems 23 and 24 treat with "arbitrariness." Can you support her claim with examples from these problems? (paragraph 1)

b. Indicate how the study of language may be, as Sargon labels it, "a science." Is any of what you have done in studying this book "scientific"? (paragraph 1) How would you describe *scientific method*?

c. What is the distinction between *a* grammar and *the* grammar? (paragraph 2) How is this related to my explanation on the first page of this book? Sargon refers to "the various kinds of grammar now being offered" and even names a few (scholarly traditional grammar, structural grammar, and transformational grammar). How is a variety of grammars possible? How is this related to my analogy of the people and the machine on page 2 of this book?

d. Distinguish between descriptiveness and prescriptiveness in a grammar. (paragraph 2)

e. Does Latin have logic and perfection in greater measure than English? (paragraph 2)

f. Must "scholarly" grammars always be based on "an exhaustive description of spoken as well as written English"? (paragraph 2) What is so important about speech?

g. Of what significance is the fact that "structural linguists collected, classified, observed stretches of physical events called utterances as the botanist collects, observes, classifies plant life"? (paragraph 3)

h. What do you suppose Sargon means in labeling meaning as "a subjective element"? (paragraph 3) Subjective though it may be, isn't meaning in language a reality? Was it justifiable for structural linguists to try "to exclude meaning" from their analysis?

i. Explain Sargon's claim that, in regard to the traditional definition of *noun*, "the native speaker unconsciously knows more than this definition tells him." (paragraph 5)

j. Are form and position, as structural linguists claim, actually reliable guides to function and meaning? (paragraph 7)

k. Does English have both *lexical meaning* and *grammatical meaning*, as Sargon claims? (paragraph 7) Can you demonstrate the two and define the division between them in the sentence "A dog bit Henry"?

l. What does Sargon's "nonsense" sequence ("A raglump propagoodle hieraddles the aleurest ptolomaniacs ptaly") demonstrate about English structure? (paragraph 8)

m. Do you agree that the real bases of our knowledge of parts of speech (noun, verb, and the like) in English and of sentence-functions (subject, modifier, and so forth) are the five devices Sargon lists: (1) inflectional endings, (2) derivational prefixes and suffixes, (3) word order, (4) associated function words, and (5) stress, pitch, and juncture? (paragraph 9)

n. Does structural grammar as Sargon outlines it really stress "inductive rather than deductive reasoning"? (paragraph 17) If so, what's so great about that?

o. Has structural grammar answered all the questions of linguistic analysis? (paragraph 21)

p. Do the theories and practices of structural grammar, as outlined in Sargon's article, point the right way to "making grammar" as far as you're concerned?

A Transformational Approach to Sentence Structure[9]

Ronald W. Langacker

Surface Structures

1)   The function of syntactic rules is to link conceptual structures [ideas] with surface structures [actual sentences]. We know very little about conceptual structures, since we know so little about human cognition in general. In comparison, the nature of surface structures is relatively easy to ascertain, and our examination of syntactic systems will consequently start with them. Although we will concentrate on English, much of the following discussion will prove valid for all languages.

2)   A sentence, as we have seen, can be segmented into a series of morphemes. *The cat scratched the dog* can be represented as *the+cat+scratch+PAST+the+dog. An old man gave the airplane to Helen* consists of the morpheme sequence *an+old+man+give+PAST+the+air+plane+to+ Helen.* The morphemes of a sentence are not randomly arranged but are combined in a very specific way to form a surface structure. We can note three aspects of the configuration of surface structures: their linear arrangement, their hierarchical arrangement, and the types of units they contain.

3)   The linear ordering of the morphemes of a sentence is self-evident. In the first string above, *the* precedes *cat* precedes *scratch* precedes *PAST,* and so on. Changing the order of the morphemes in a sentence results either in an ungrammatical string or in another sentence. *Cat the dog the scratched,* for instance, is an ungrammatical string. *The*

[9] Excerpted from *Language and Its Structure: Some Fundamental Linguistic Concepts,* 2nd edition, by Ronald W. Langacker, copyright © 1967, 1968, 1973, by Harcourt Brace Jovanovich, Inc., and reprinted with their permission.

dog scratched the cat is grammatical, but it is simply not the same sentence as *The cat scratched the dog.*

4)   The morphemes of a sentence are also arranged hierarchically. We observed earlier that the morphemes of *The cat scratched the dog* cohere to form larger units. *The* and *cat* function as a group in some sense, whereas *PAST* and *the* in no way stand apart from the rest of the string as a unit. A string of morphemes that constitutes such a unit is called a **constituent.** *The+cat* is thus a constituent of *The cat scratched the dog,* but *PAST+the* is not.

5)   The entire string *the+cat+scratch+PAST+the+dog* can be considered a constituent, since it constitutes a special kind of unit, a sentence. This string can be broken down into two smaller constituents, *the+cat* and *scratch+PAST+the +dog,* and the latter has the subconstituents *scratch+PAST* and *the+dog.* Finally, each individual morpheme is a constituent. . . .

Constituent Types

6)   We have not said everything there is to say about a surface structure when we have described the linear ordering of its morphemes and their hierarchical arrangement. . . . Certain morpheme sequences belong together as constituents and others do not. . . . *The cat* and *the dog* are constituents of the same kind, as opposed to, say, *scratched* or *will come.* . . . *Steve or Sam and Bob, an old man* and *the dog* are similar. . . . *will come, gave the airplane to Helen,* and *scratched the dog* are similar, but . . . *an old man* and *scratched the dog* are constituents of different types. . . .

7)   We see . . . that a single-word noun like *Helen* can function as a noun phrase as well as more complex structures such as *an old man* or *Steve or Sam and Bob.* Similarly, a verb phrase may consist of just a verb, like *exists,* or it may be more complex, like *gave the airplane to Helen.* The reason why such diverse structures as *Helen, an old man,* and *Steve or Sam and Bob* are labeled as the same type of constituent is that they behave alike with respect to syntactic rules. To take just one example, consider the rule for forming questions in English. In a question, the first verb word precedes the noun-phrase subject; this contrasts with

the usual word order, in which the verb follows the subject. The question form of *Helen will come*, therefore, is *Will Helen come?*, the order of *Helen* and *will* being the opposite of their noninterrogative order. In the same way, the question form of *An old man will come* is *Will an old man come?*, and that of *Steve or Sam and Bob will come* is *Will Steve or Sam and Bob come?* In each case, the question differs from the noninterrogative sentence only in the relative order of *will* and the string of morphemes said to be a noun phrase. Since *Helen, an old man,* and *Steve or Sam and Bob* function alike with respect to the rule of question formation, and with respect to many other syntactic rules of English besides, we are justified in treating them as constituents of the same type.

8)   One should not conclude that surface structures are fully understood. . . . Nevertheless, some things are fairly clear: the morphemes of a sentence are arranged in a hierarchical structure of some kind, the major outlines of which can be sketched with reasonable assurance, and we must identify types of constituents by labeling or by some comparable device.

Complex Sentences

9)   The powers of human conceptualization enable us (in principle at least) to form thoughts of any desired degree of complexity. Regardless of how complex a conceptual structure may be, the syntactic rules and lexical choices of a language allow us to construct a grammatical sentence to represent it. The grammatical sentences of a language thus form an infinite set, since there is no intrinsic limit to the length or complexity of the meaningful sentences that the grammar of a language specifies to be well formed. In this section, we will examine more closely those aspects of syntactic systems which project our linguistic competence to an infinite set of sentences.

Complex Conceptual Structures

10)   Sentences, like the thoughts they represent, vary greatly in complexity. *Pete fainted* is a simpler sentence than *Alice broke the fancy chamber pot which had been given to her*

by her great-aunt, in terms of both conceptual and surface structure. The latter sentence is in turn less complex than *Linguists are no different from any other people who spend more than nineteen hours a day pondering the complexities of grammar and its relationship to practically everything else in order to prove that language is so inordinately complicated that it is impossible in principle for people to talk.*

11)   We are concerned here with a special kind of complexity. Specifically, many sentences are complex in the sense that they are constructed out of simpler ones. For example, *I believe Shirley hopes the rattlesnake bit me* can be decomposed into the simpler sentences *I believe, Shirley hopes,* and *The rattlesnake bit me.* By combining with *but* the simple sentences *Eggplant turns me on* and *Rhubarb nauseates me,* we obtain the more complex sentence *Eggplant turns me on, but rhubarb nauseates me.* Traditionally, the simple sentence-like components that go into the construction of complex sentences are known as **clauses;** a clause, roughly defined, is a constituent that contains a verbal element of some kind and could (perhaps with slight modification) stand alone as an independent sentence. We can therefore define a **complex sentence** as one that consists of more than one clause.

12)   By and large, the clauses of a complex sentence correspond to components of the underlying conceptual structure. Thus the conceptual structure of *Eggplant turns me on, but rhubarb nauseates me* involves two main propositions, one pertaining to the speaker's reaction to eggplant, and the other his reaction to rhubarb. These propositions correspond directly to the two surface clauses *eggplant turns me on* and *rhubarb nauseates me.* Similarly, the semantic structure of *I believe Shirley hopes the rattlesnake bit me* contains three main components that correspond directly to surface clauses. One component pertains to a belief on the speaker's part, the second to a hope on Shirley's part, and the third to the biting of the speaker by the rattlesnake.

13)   The correlation between surface clauses and components of meaning is at best imperfect, however. While the surface clauses of a complex sentence almost invariably correspond to semantic propositions, not every semantic proposition is realized as a separate clause in surface structure. For example, consider the sentence *Pete fainted after*

the nurse took his temperature. The conceptual structure
of this sentence involves at least three separate propositions: that Pete fainted, that the nurse took his temperature,
and that the first of these events followed the second. But the
sentence contains only two surface clauses: *Pete fainted*
and *after the nurse took his temperature.* The single word
after conveys the meaning of one proposition; this word
is part of a clause, but it is not a clause in its own right. The
same is true of the adjective *black* in the sentence *A black
dog bit him.* This sentence has only one clause in surface
structure, but semantically it is complex, since it involves
two propositions: that a dog bit him, and that the dog was
black.

14)   Some components in the conceptual structures of sentences have no direct surface realization at all. This is true,
for instance, in the imperative sentence *Open the crypt at
once!* It is part of the meaning of this sentence that the
speaker is giving a command to the hearer, but the sentence
has no surface clause, such as *I order you,* that expresses
this meaning directly. Nor is there any lexical item present
with that meaning. The sense of *I order you* must be deduced by the hearer on the basis of the form of the sentence
(it lacks an overt subject), its intonation, and the context.
Interrogative sentences provide another example. In a question such as *Does she really have fleas?* there is no surface
clause that directly expresses the sense of *I ask you,* yet it is
intuitively clear that this sense is part of the conceptual
structure of the sentence. Once again, the interrogative
force of the sentence must be deduced from its form (the
subject follows the auxiliary verb *does*), its intonation, and
the context.

15)   We see, then, that the conceptual structures of sentences
are often more complex than their surface structures would
indicate. Semantic components that could be expressed
as separate clauses sometimes surface instead as smaller
units, or have no direct surface realization at all. In fact, it
is not unreasonable to speculate that every sentence has a
complex conceptual structure with more than one component proposition, even though many sentences are non-
complex on the surface. It has been suggested, for instance,
that the conceptual structure of every sentence involves a
specification (such as *I order you, I ask you,* or *I say to you*)

of the type of **speech act** it represents, even though this specification often fails to surface as a separate clause. It has also been suggested that specifications of tense (that is, the location of an event in time relative to the time of utterance) constitute separate propositions at the level of semantic structure. If these suggestions are correct, even the simplest sentence can be analyzed as consisting semantically of several propositions. And a simple, everyday sentence like *Three small wombats sneezed,* with only one surface clause, has at least five propositions in its conceptual structure: that the speaker is making a statement (as opposed to asking a question or giving a command), that sneezing is being predicated of wombats, that the event of sneezing is located in the past, that the wombats were small, and that there were three of them.

16) Let us now return to the observation that some sentences are complex in the sense that they are constructed out of simpler ones. Taken informally, this statement is correct and expresses a fundamental insight about the nature of sentence structure. When we say that the sentence *I believe Shirley hopes the rattlesnake bit me* is constructed out of the simpler sentences *I believe, Shirley hopes,* and *The rattlesnake bit me,* we are correctly characterizing certain aspects of its syntactic structure. . . . Clauses are conceived of as simple sentences used in the construction of more complex ones.

17) Strictly speaking, however, this conception is misleading in certain respects. For one thing, it pertains mainly to surface structure. In terms of surface form, *I believe Shirley hopes the rattlesnake bit me* does consist of the simpler structures *I believe, Shirley hopes,* and *The rattlesnake bit me,* but we have seen that surface form is only one aspect of the structure of a sentence. In terms of conceptual structure, the relation is not so simple; by merely combining the conceptual structures of the simple sentences *I believe, Shirley hopes, and The rattlesnake bit me,* we do not obtain that of the complex sentence. Notice, for example, that it is part of the meaning of *The rattlesnake bit me* that the speaker is asserting the truth of this state of affairs—the speaker would be insincere if he uttered the sentence while believing that he had not in fact been bitten by the rattlesnake. But this is not part of the meaning of *I believe Shirley*

hopes the rattlesnake bit me. A speaker could utter the latter sentence with perfect sincerity even if he knew for a fact that the rattlesnake had not bitten him.

18)   The notion that complex sentences are constructed out of simpler ones is somewhat misleading even in terms of surface structure, for the following reason. When a clause functions as part of a complex sentence, it is often modified by special syntactic rules and thereby assumes a form that it could not have were it to occur alone as a complete and independent sentence. For example, the clause *trolls hate water* may stand alone as an independent sentence, or it may function as part of a more complex sentence, perhaps as the subject of *is obvious.* If *trolls hate water* is used as the subject of *is obvious* in a complex sentence, a syntactic rule of English requires that it be preceded by the subordinator *that: That trolls hate water is obvious.* The clause must occur with *that* when used in the complex sentence, and it may not occur with *that* when used in isolation as an independent sentence (*Trolls hate water is obvious* and *That trolls hate water* are both ungrammatical sentences). Because of the syntactic principles of English, therefore, this clause differs in surface form depending on whether it stands alone or is incorporated in a more elaborate structure.

19)   Relative clauses provide another example. (A relative clause is one that modifies a noun phrase.) Consider the sentence *Joan distracted the man to whom Marge was speaking.* This sentence consists of two clauses which, were they to occur alone as independent sentences, would have the form *Marge was speaking to a man* and *Joan distracted the man.* The first of these is used as a relative clause modifying *the man* in the second, and because it functions as a relative clause, its form is modified by various syntactic rules of English. Specifically, the prepositional phrase *to a man* occurs at the beginning of the clause instead of after the verb, and the relative pronoun *whom* replaces the noun phrase *a man* as the object of the preposition *to. To whom Marge was speaking* is not grammatical as an independent sentence, nor does *Marge was speaking to a man* constitute a well-formed relative clause.

20)   In summary, all sentences are probably complex at the level of conceptual structure, being decomposable into com-

ponent propositions. Individual propositions of a conceptual structure have varying surface manifestations as determined by syntactic rules and lexical choices; a proposition may surface as a clause, it may be manifested as some
smaller unit, or it may have no direct surface realization at
all. Because of these syntactic and lexical modifications,
the surface structure of a sentence tends to be simpler than
its conceptual structure and to conceal the true complexity
of the latter. Some semantically complex sentences thus
consist of only one surface clause. Others are complex in
surface structure as well, consisting of multiple surface
clauses that reflect components of the underlying semantic
structure. When a clause is used in the construction of a
complex sentence, it is often modified by syntactic rules that
would not apply were it to stand alone as a simple sentence.
For this reason, the clauses of a complex sentence are not
always identical to the simple sentences from which (informally speaking) the complex sentence is constructed.

Conjoining

21)   In traditional grammar, a distinction is made between
coordination and **subordination.** The clauses of a complex
sentence are said to be in a relation of coordination when
they have "equal rank," as in *The sparrow is flighty, and
the lion is a beast.* Otherwise they are said to be in a relation
of subordination. In the sentence *It is obvious that trolls
hate water,* for example, *it is obvious* functions as the **main**
clause, while *that trolls hate water* constitutes a **subordinate**
clause.

22)   . . . The surface structure of *The sparrow is flighty,
and the lion is a beast . . .* is constructed by combining
with *and* the clauses *the sparrow is flighty* and *the lion is a
beast.* Since this is a coordinate structure, the two component clauses are arranged "in parallel"—neither contains
the other as a constituent. The two clauses are said to be
conjoined, and each clause is a **conjunct** of the conjoined
structure. Elements like *and,* which connect the conjuncts
of a conjoined structure, are called **conjunctions.** . . .

23)   There is no intrinsic limit on the number of conjuncts
a coordinate structure can have. By adding a third clause to

the example, we obtain the longer sentence *The sparrow is flighty, and the lion is a beast, and the doe is a dear;* by adding a fourth conjunct, we obtain the still longer sentence *The sparrow is flighty, and the lion is a beast, and the doe is a dear, and the caterpillar is a creep;* and so on. It should be evident that we could continue the process indefinitely, for length alone never renders such a sentence ungrammatical. For this reason the process of conjoining is itself sufficient to extend our linguistic competence to an infinite set of sentences. . . .

24)   *And* is of course only one of the conjunctions of English. The other two major conjunctions are *but* and *or*, illustrated in the following sentences: *All men are equal, but some are more equal than others; Get your hair cut at once, or at least buy a hair-net! And, or,* and *but* also combine with other words to form more complex conjunctions, such as *either . . . or, both . . . and, but then, or else,* and so on. The simple conjunctions can occur before every conjunct in a conjoined structure, as the earlier examples showed, with the exception that they may not occur before the first conjunct. A sentence like *And she is beautiful, and she is charming* is therefore ungrammatical (except in special contexts where it continues a previous enumeration), since *and* incorrectly appears before the first conjunct, *she is beautiful.* Notice that the English conjunctions are more closely bound to the following conjunct than to the preceding one, as shown by the greater naturalness of pausing before a conjunction than after it: compared to *Penelope is very shy —and Abernathy is too,* with the pause before *and,* the sentence *Penelope is very shy and—Abernathy is too* sounds very awkward and unnatural. . . .

25)   Various syntactic principles affect the surface manifestation of coordinate structures. For example, one syntactic rule of English allows the omission of all but the last occurrence of *and* or *or* in a series of conjuncts. This principle allows *The sparrow is flighty, the lion is a beast, the doe is a dear, and the caterpillar is a creep* as a variant of the fuller sentence *The sparrow is flighty, and the lion is a beast, and the doe is a dear, and the caterpillar is a creep.* (This rule can never affect sentences conjoined with *but,* since *but* is restricted to cases where there are only two conjuncts.)

26)   More drastic in their effect are various rules that sim-

plify conjuncts by deleting repeated elements. For instance, the verbs of all conjuncts except the first may be deleted if the verbs of all the conjuncts are identical (and if certain other conditions are met). From the structure *Jane munched on snails, Joyce munched on roasted grasshoppers, and Julie munched on chocolate-covered caterpillars,* this rule produces the optional variant *Jane munched on snails, Joyce on roasted grasshoppers, and Julie on chocolate-covered caterpillars.* Another rule permits the deletion of everything but the subject and auxiliary verb in the second conjunct when the remainder is identical to the corresponding elements in the first conjunct. This rule determines the surface form of sentences like these: *Wilt can break a railroad tie with his bare hands, and Nate can also; Penelope is very shy, and Abernathy is too; Uranium will not dissolve in Coca-Cola, but teeth will; The linebacker should make the tackle, or else the safety should. Break a railroad tie with his bare hands, very shy, dissolve in Coca-Cola,* and *make the tackle* have been deleted from the second conjuncts of these respective sentences.

27)   Thus far we have concerned ourselves only with conjoined clauses, but smaller constituents can also be conjoined. For example, *the cruiser and the old battleship* is a conjoined noun phrase formed by combining the simpler noun phrases *the cruiser* and *the old battleship. . . .* The coordination of other types of constituents (verbs, adjectives, verb phrases, and prepositions) is illustrated in the following sentences: *She bit and scratched the mugger; I want to marry a man who is tall, dark, handsome, and rich; Alexander believes that all non-patriots should leave the country and thinks that anyone who casts aspersion on the flag should be shot immediately; She slid up and down the bannister.*

28)   There is reason to believe that many instances of conjoined constituents other than clauses are best regarded as reduced versions of conjoined clauses. Consider, for example, the sentence *The cruiser and the old battleship need painting.* In surface structure, this sentence consists of only one clause and has a conjoined noun phrase subject. In terms of meaning, however, it is equivalent to the complex sentence *The cruiser needs painting, and the old battleship needs painting,* which consists of two conjoined

clauses. Thus it is not unreasonable to claim that the two sentences derive from the same complex conceptual structure. The second sentence reflects this conceptual structure fairly directly, but the first is modified by syntactic rules that delete the identical elements (*needs painting*) from one of the conjuncts and combine the two subjects, *the cruiser* and *the old battleship*, to form a conjoined subject. A similar analysis might be proposed for other sentences. Thus *She bit and scratched the mugger* can be regarded as a variant of *She bit the mugger and she scratched the mugger; I want to marry a man who is tall, dark, handsome, and rich* may be derived from the same conceptual structure as *I want to marry a man who is tall, who is dark, who is handsome, and who is rich;* and so on.

29)   There are, however, sentences for which such an analysis appears to be inappropriate. For example, *John and Marsha met in New York* is certainly not equivalent to *John met in New York, and Marsha met in New York;* the latter, in fact, is semantically anomalous. By the same token, *We painted the football red, white, and blue all over* does not derive from the same conceptual structure as *We painted the football red all over, we painted the football white all over, and we painted the football blue all over.* Therefore, even if one accepts the hypothesis that conjoined clauses may be reduced by syntactic rules to single clauses containing smaller conjoined constituents, it is still dubious that all instances of conjoined constituents other than clauses arise in this way.

Embedding

30)   In a coordinate structure . . . , none of the conjoined clauses is contained in any other; by definition, the component clauses are all on a par. When one clause does function as a constituent of another, we speak instead of a relation of subordination. The subordinate clause is said to be **embedded** in the main clause.

31)   The subordinate status of a clause is quite apparent when it functions as the subject or object of another clause. Such a clause is referred to as a **complement** clause. For example, *that trolls hate water* functions as the subject of *is obvious* in the sentence *That trolls hate water is obvious.*

. . . The structure of this sentence is quite analogous to that of *The answer is obvious,* except that the subject happens to be a clause rather than a simple article-noun combination. Evidence for analyzing this subject clause as a noun phrase is provided by the fact that it shares many (though not all) syntactic properties with clearly nominal constituents such as *the answer.* Notice, for instance, that both *the answer* and *that trolls hate water* can respond to the question word *what: What is obvious? The answer is obvious; What is obvious? That trolls hate water is obvious.* Moreover, the pronoun *it* can refer back to either one: *The answer is obvious, isn't it? Yes, it is obvious; That trolls hate water is obvious, isn't it? Yes, it is obvious.*

32)   The subordinate status of **relative clauses** is also quite apparent. . . . [In the sentence] *Irving ruined the company which he inherited* . . . the relative clause *which he inherited* is embedded in the main clause *Irving ruined the company* and modifies its direct-object noun phrase, *the company.* . . . The relative clause and the nominal it modifies combine to form a more complex noun-phrase object, *the company which he inherited.* . . . *The company which he inherited* bears the same relation to *ruined* that *my watch* does in the simple sentence *Irving ruined my watch*—namely, both expressions are objects. It is not difficult to find evidence that supports this claim. For instance, the active sentence *Irving ruined my watch* has the passive variant *My watch was ruined by Irving;* the direct-object noun phrase *my watch* in the active sentence occurs as the surface subject in the passive variant. *The company which he inherited* functions just like *my watch* with respect to passivization: *The company which he inherited was ruined by Irving.* . . .

33)   There are many kinds of subordinate clauses in addition to relative and complement clauses, though it is not possible to deal with them systematically here. They include: **adverbial clauses of time or location,** typically marked by subordinators such as *when, while,* and *where* (*When we got there, the door was ajar; While doing push-ups, Felicita makes strange, grunting noises; Where I work, it is hard to find a parking space*); **clauses specifying reason or intent,** headed by subordinators such as *because, since,* and *in order to* (*Because she had a headache, I took my date home*

early; Since we were trailing by 37 runs in the eighth inning, I let my sister play; In order to appear calm for the interview, he guzzled down three quarts of Scotch); and many others (for example: *Although she was rich, she was very happy indeed; Tom can mix martinis faster than Jerry can drink margaritas; Mars exploded, which led certain astronomers to the conclusion that it must have been inhabited by human-like creatures; They chose George to be the new sex symbol*).

34)   The various devices for embedding one clause in another are like conjunction in that they extend our linguistic competence to an infinite set of sentences. A subordinate clause embedded in a main clause to form a complex sentence may itself be complex, consisting of a main and subordinate clause; this new subordinate clause may in turn contain another one, which in turn contains another; and so on.

Questions about "A Transformational Approach to Sentence Structure"

Below are questions to assist you in analyzing Langacker's essay.

a. Why do we know very little about conceptual structures but much more about surface structures? (paragraph 1)

b. What is meant by the statement that "the morphemes of a sentence are . . . arranged hierarchically"? (paragraph 4)

c. Explain the idea that "the grammatical sentences of a language . . . form an infinite set." (paragraph 9)

d. What is a "well formed" sentence? (paragraph 9)

e. If the sentences of a language form "an infinite set," how can human beings comprehend so many sentences? (paragraph 9)

f. In connection with question *e* above, what is the significance of the theory that "many sentences are complex in the sense that they are constructed out of simpler ones"? (paragraph 11)

g. Explain the idea of "surface realization" of "conceptual structures." (paragraph 14)

h. What is the meaning of the claim that "the conceptual structure of sentences are often more complex than their surface structures would indicate"? (paragraph 15)

i. What are "semantic components"? (paragraph 15)

j. Explain: "When a clause functions as part of a complex sentence, it is often modified by special syntactic rules and thereby assumes a form that it could not have were it to occur alone as a complete and independent sentence." (paragraph 18)

k. In what ways are "many instances of conjoined constituents other than clauses . . . best regarded as reduced versions of conjoined clauses"? (paragraph 28)

l. What is "embedding"? (paragraph 30)

m. What elements of structural grammar as defined in Sargon's article "The Structural Revolution" are present in Langacker's transformational analysis?

n. What concepts are present in Langacker's analysis of sentences but not in Sargon's?

o. In what ways is a transformational analysis of sentences such as Langacker's related to psychological study?

p. What are the defining characteristics of a transformational grammar as represented by Langacker's account?

B. EVALUATING GRAMMAR

1. Most linguists agree that the main goal of a grammar of English is to explain how people understand and produce English sentences. They further agree that transformational grammar is the present theory which offers the most promising basis for reaching this goal.

In light of your knowledge of traditional, structural, and transformational theory, do you agree or disagree?

2. Write an essay in which you state your answer and fully explain the reasoning behind it.

C. GRAMMAR AND PEOPLE

1. "Grammar and People"—now, we're really face-to-face with the question of the relevance of *grammar* (as explanation of the system of language) to people's use of language in everyday life.

Is there any relevance?

problem 26

The value of grammatical study

No subdivisions here at all. Just a simple little way of ending a big book. But not an insignificant way.

Although there are many aspects to the system of the English language in addition to the ones we've covered in this book, still we've been over a lot of ground together, making grammar.

Was it all worth the effort?

As a closing gesture, please write out your ideas on either or both of the following items:

a. the benefits of studying the system of the English language and of making grammar
b. the reasons against studying the system of the English language and of making grammar

Some more technicalities

After the overview of the system of the English language presented in problems 1 to 9, I catalogued and explained in the section entitled "Getting Technical" some of the relevant technical terms used by linguists—just in case you were interested or might need them. This section contains additional technical terms, which relate to the material in Problems 10 to 22.

PROBLEM 10. A visual symbol for a phoneme is called a *grapheme*. In English, a grapheme is one or more letters of the alphabet. A.9 lists nineteen graphemes for /i/, for example.

PROBLEM 11. The special alphabet introduced in A.2 is known as a *phonemic alphabet*. (Some people call it a *phonetic alphabet*; but, technically, it is not.)

The process of sound-change discussed in A.3 is *phonetic assimilation*. This is the process of one sound affecting another; strictly speaking, one sound assimilates to another—that is, changes to become more like the other. The specific kind covered here is *voice-assimilation,* in which one sound which does not have the vibration (*voice*) adds it to become like an adjacent sound which has it; or one sound with it loses it to become like the other which does not have it.

The various plural suffixes treated in A.5 are called *allomorphs*. An allomorph is one of the variants of a single morpheme; they mean the same thing but don't sound alike.

In addition to examples of assimilation, A.10 treats *epenthesis*

175

(the insertion of an extra sound, as in /səmpθɪŋ/), *metathesis* (reversal as in *relevant*), and *epithesis* (addition of an extra consonant at the end, as in *acrosst*).

PROBLEM 12. The groups of words which will fit the blanks in the sentences in A.2, 8, and 14 are called *position classes*. Words which have characteristic forms, as those in 3, 9, 15, and 18 are members of *form-classes*. *Position-classes* are broader categories; not all words which can fill the same slot have the same forms. The name for the position class illustrated in 2 is *nominal*; the form-class given in 3 is *noun* (or *Form Class I*). The position class in 8 is *adjectival*; the form-class in 9 is *adjective* (*Form Class III*). The position class in 14 is *adverbial*; the form-class in 15, *adverb* (*Form Class IV*). *Verbs*, treated in 18, are also called *Form Class II*; their position is called *verbal*.

PROBLEM 13. The words treated in this problem are members of *structure* or *function classes*, except for pronouns, which are usually considered a subclass of nouns.

The question raised in A.3.b deals with the distinction between *open* and *closed* classes or words. Nouns, verbs, adjectives, and adverbs are open classes—they are open to new members; the others are closed.

Nouns, verbs, adjectives, and adverbs are also called *content words* as opposed to *structure* or *function words*.

Exercises 5 and 6 deal with *connecting words*, which is a poor term. *But* and other words like it are traditionally called *coordinating conjunctions*; *although* and words like it are *subordinating conjunctions*; and *however* and words like it are called *conjunctive adverbs*. Though the three groups have some distinct differences, the names are not at all indicative of these differences.

Exercises 7 to 9 treat *auxiliary verbs* (also called *helping verbs*); recently, they have been called simply *auxiliaries*.

Exercise 10 deals with *noun-markers* (also called *noun-determiners*). Exercise 11 deals with *intensifiers* or *qualifiers*.

PROBLEM 14. Numerous terms have been used to distinguish the groups of words treated in A.1 to 9. *The* and other words like it are mentioned in the preceding paragraph as *noun-markers*. *Red* and *ugly* and similar words are usually called *descriptive adjectives* (sometimes just *adjectives*). *Metal* and similar words are sometimes called *material adjectives,* other times *noun adjuncts,* which, like *floor,* are nouns used to modify other nouns. *Oscillating* is a *participle,* specifically a *present participle.* All the classes mentioned here are *prenominal modifiers,* though, under certain conditions, some may follow nouns.

The positional distinction between adjectives as covered in 14.C.3 is usually labeled with the terms *attributive adjective* (before the noun) and *predicate adjective* (after a *be* or linking verb).

PROBLEM 15. A.6 deals with *tense,* a term which, in modern usage, is limited to the present and past forms of the first item in a verb phrase. Modern linguists usually do not use other tense-names.

The *-ing* form of a verb (*singing*) is, as mentioned with the terms for problem 14, called the *present participle.* Forms such as *sung* and *pinched* in *has sung* and *has pinched* are called *past participles.*

PROBLEM 16. In connection with A.4, the terms *direct object* to denote the second noun and *indirect object* to denote the first are traditional. For a while in the 1950s and 1960s, they were unpopular among linguists; but they are widely used nowadays, though they are not very meaningful names.

PROBLEM 17. The transformations covered here are known as *nominalizing transformations* (*nominalizations*). In traditional terminology, structures such as "that Marvin was a screwball" (A.2) are called *noun clauses,* clauses functioning as nouns. "Bess to wear a wig" is an *infinitive phrase,* a phrase headed by *to* + the uninflected verb-form; used as a noun, it may be referred to as a *nominal infinitive phrase* (or just *noun infinitive phrase*). "Mary Helen's murdering her father" (A.10), a participial phrase used as a noun, is called a *gerund.* Constructions like "the well having gone dry" (exercise B) are called *nominative absolutes.*

In connection with 17.C.5, there is a new area of study called *psycholinguistics.*

PROBLEM 18. The transformational process examined here is *deletion.* The main condition for deletions (A.4) is that the items deleted must be *easily recoverable items,* that is, items which are conventionally deleted and, therefore, known to or recoverable by any speaker of the language.

The sentences discussed in A.6 are *imperatives,* sentences which denote orders and which do not have explicit subjects.

PROBLEM 19. The concept of underlying sentences treated in A.2 to 10 is the concept of *deep structure* in transformational grammar. It is the theoretical construction which contains all elements of the meaning of a sentence whether or not they are explicit in the sentence as it is actually spoken or written. The actual sentence is called a *surface structure.*

PROBLEM 20. This problem deals with *semantics,* the analysis of lexical meaning. A.14 to 20 cover *semantic features,* the items which constitute the meaning of a word.

PROBLEM 21. *Figurative language,* which is treated here, is often defined as "non-literal use of language"; but, as the exercises in this problem suggest, this is not a very exact definition. In addition, it must be noted that there is a tacit understanding between the user and the audience that the language is not literal and that it is used for effect.

The *figures of speech* in A.8 are *metaphors,* comparisons of unlike items implied, not stated explicitly. (If the comparison is stated explicitly—"My luve is *like* a red, red rose"—the figure is called a *simile.*) Literary exaggeration (A.10) is called *hyperbole* (or *overstatement*); *understatement* (exercise 11) is technically known as *litotes.* The statements cited in A.12 are examples of *irony of statement,* which is a statement that is intended to mean the opposite of what its words literally denote.

PROBLEM 22. The nonlinguistic accompaniments to speech treated here are sometimes called *paralanguage,* a term which simply means "above or outside language." The study of paralanguage is *paralinguistics.* Gestures and facial expressions are popularly known as *body language.*